MW01609935

Trading for Beginners

The Ultimate Guide to Make Money Online with Options and Forex Trading. Discover the Benefits of Technical Analysis, Financial Leverage and Risk Management to Generate Passive Income

[Samuel Douglas]

Legal & Disclaimer

The information contained in this book and its contents is not designed to replace or take the place of any form of medical or professional advice; and is not meant to replace the need for independent medical, financial, legal or other professional advice or services, as may be required. The content and information in this book has been provided for educational and entertainment purposes only.

The content and information contained in this book has been compiled from sources deemed reliable, and it is accurate to the best of the Author's knowledge, information and belief. However, the Author cannot guarantee its accuracy and validity and cannot be held liable for any errors and/or omissions. Further, changes are periodically made to this book as and when needed. Where appropriate and/or necessary, you must consult a professional (including but not limited to your doctor, attorney, financial advisor or such other professional advisor) before using any of the suggested remedies, techniques, or information in this book.

Upon using the contents and information contained in this book, you agree to hold harmless the Author from and against any damages, costs, and expenses, including any legal fees potentially resulting from the application of any of the information provided by this book. This disclaimer applies to any loss, damages or injury caused by the use and application, whether directly or indirectly, of any advice or information presented, whether for breach of contract, tort, negligence, personal injury, criminal intent, or under any other cause of action.

You agree to accept all risks of using the information presented inside this book.

You agree that by continuing to read this book, where appropriate and/or necessary, you shall consult a professional (including but not limited to your doctor, attorney, or financial advisor or such other advisor as needed) before using any of the suggested remedies, techniques, or information in this book.

Table of Contents

INTRODUCTION

The foreign exchange market, or Forex market, is a fast-paced and exciting market. Until recently, this kind of trading was only done by central banks, corporations, financial institutions, and wealthy individuals. But thanks to the emergence of the internet, many more people can join the market and use it to do investing as well.

Daily currency fluctuations are going to be small. Most pairs of currencies are only going to move about a cent each day, which will represent a change that is less than 1 percent in the value of the currency. This means that in most cases, the Forex market is going to be one of the least volatile financial markets around. Therefore, many currency speculators are going to rely on enormous amounts of leverage to increase how valuable a potential movement can be. In fact, with the Forex market, the leverage can be as high as 250:1.

This leverage is really high and can be really risky. But because of the deep amount of liquidity and the fact that the Forex market is available to be traded around the clock, many brokers can make high leverage the standard of the industry which can make the movements more meaningful for most currency traders.

Extreme liquidity and the high leverage of this market has really helped to push rapid growth in the market, making it a great place for investing with many traders. Positions on this market can be opened, and then closed again, within minutes, or the trader can choose to hold onto the position for months. Currency prices are going to be based on the idea of supply and demand or that currency pair at the time, and it is hard to manipulate them easily, simply because the size of the market is just so big. Even central banks and other large players in the market are not able to make changes that will move the prices of currency pairs as well.

While many of the players in the Forex market are going to be larger players like banks and financial institutions, there are still opportunities for investors to get in. However, for the individual to do well, they need to know some of the basics of any movements in the currency, or they are going to run into trouble and will lose more money than they can gain on this market.

This means that the importer in the United States would have to take their USD and then exchange it out for euros so that they can pay for the cheese (or any other product depending on what they work on. The same will go for traveling and so much more. If you wish to leave the United States and go to Egypt, you will have to change your money into the one that is the locally accepted currency before you can purchase anything there.

The need to exchange these currencies is one of the biggest reasons why this is the largest and the most liquid financial market in the world. It is so huge because it has to deal with all the currencies that are present in the world. It is estimated that the average value that is traded on this forum is $2,000 billion each day (based on the USD). The total volume is going to change each day though, and it is likely that this number will keep going up.

One unique aspect of this particular market is that there isn't a central marketplace for this exchange. Instead, the currency is going to be conducted electronically over the counter. What this means is that all of the transactions that occur with the Forex market is going to occur via computers and between traders that are around the world, rather than with one centralized exchange like what happens with the stock market.

The Forex market is going to be open 24 hours a day, five and a half days a week, and the currencies can be traded at all the financial centers throughout the world. With so many different countries on the market, it is possible that the market is starting brand new in Hong Kong and Tokyo when it is ending for the day with the United States. This is why the Forex market has the potential to be active at any time of the day, and the price quotes on currencies are likely to change all of the time.

These include the spot market, the futures market, and the forwards market. The forex trading with the spot market is often the largest because it is the underlying real asset that the futures and the forwards market are based on. Traditionally, the futures market was the most popular because it stayed open for longer times with individual investors. But thanks to electronic trading and more Forex brokers, more people have started to go with the spot market.

The spot market is where the currencies are going to be bought or sold based on their current price. The price that you can buy or sell the currencies at will be determined by supply and demand and can reflect a lot of different things including political situations, economic performance, interest rates, and more.

This is going to be a bilateral transaction where one party is going to deliver an amount for the currency that is agreed upon to the counterparty, and then they will receive a specified amount of another currency at the exchange rate value. After the position is closed, the settlement is going to be in cash. Although this is the market that is known for dealing with transactions that happen in the present, rather than in the future, it does take about two days for the settlement to get done.

Then there is also the futures and forwards market. Unlike with the spot market, these two markets aren't going to trade actual currencies. Instead, they are going to deal with contracts that represent claims to a certain currency type of a specific price per unit, and a future date for settlement. With the forwards market, the contracts will be bought and then sold over the counter for both parties. These two parties get to decide the terms of that agreement on their own.

But with the futures market, contracts are going to be bought and then sold based on a standard size and settlement date and will occur on the market for public commodities. For these, the National Futures Association in the United States will regulate this kind of market. These contracts are going to have more specifics with them, including how many units the parties will trade, the delivery as well as the settlement dates, the minimum price increments, and more. These all need to be determined ahead of time to make sure everyone is on the same page.

There are a lot of benefits of working in the Forex market, which makes it the perfect choice when you are looking for new investment to help you out. Some of the benefits that come with trading in the Forex market include:

- It is open 24-hours a day: This is a worldwide trading platform, which means that there is going to be a market open somewhere, even if it's not in your own country.

- High Liquidity: Liquidity is the ability of any asset to quickly be converted over into cash, without a price discount. What this means in Forex is that you can move your money into and out of the market with very little price movement.

- Costs for the transactions are low: The cost of a transaction will often be put into the price with Forex, and it is known as the spread. The spread will be the difference between your purchase and your selling price. Having lower costs for transactions can do wonders when it comes to helping you to save money and put more of your profits on investment back into your pocket.

- You can use leverage: Forex brokers do allow their traders to use leverage. Leverage is basically the ability to trade some extra money on the market than what you have in your account. This helps you to make some bigger trades but can be risky to accomplish as well.

- Lots of options: If you are first looking at the Forex market, it is likely that you will see a lot of options available. You can pick from a wide variety of currency pairs. And while many people feel like they should stick with some of the major pairs when they first get started to help them gain familiarity with the market, it is also possible to try out some different matches of currency pairs based on what you read in the market and what interest you the most. Everyone can join the Forex market and see some success simply because there are so many options and it is possible to earn money no matter where the currencies go, as long as you made the right predictions.

These are just some of the benefits that can come with working in the Forex market. There are also a few negatives that you will need to watch out for. For example, while the Forex market is one that is open 24-hours a day, this can also be a negative because a short move may happen when you aren't able to watch the screen. No one can sit around and watch the market all the time so this can lead to some positions not going the way that you want. You need to make sure that you pick currencies that will stay stable, even overnight, because no one can watch the market all the time.

Also, while the transaction costs are going to be lower on this market compared to others, there can be issues if you end up trading too much. If you trade all the time, the costs are still going to add up, and they may not be enough to help you see the results that you want or cover the profits as they should. For the most part, it is best to go with

6

a long-term investing strategy because you only have to pay for the transactions once and then you can enjoy the profits when it is time to take out.

Before you enter the market, make sure that both of the currencies in your currency pair are liquid enough. If one currency pair doesn't have the right amount of liquidity, it can become very difficult to sell that position later on. The more liquidity that both of the currencies have in your pair, the easier it is to buy and sell them and do your trades.

Always watch out for the idea of leverage. Yes, this does allow you to have a stronger position when you enter because you get to work with more capital than you would in other situations. But this can be a really dangerous mindset to get into. Using more capital than you have to do a trade can increase your risk and may make it, so you lose a ton of money. Until you become more familiar with the Forex market, it is best to just stick with the capital that you can afford to lose, rather than relying on leverage. This helps you make strong and sound decisions, without going over your head.

There is so much to love about the Forex market. There are many different currency pairs that you can work with, the market is open all the time, there are many ways to make profits, and so much more. This is definitely a type of investment that can work out well for many investors, whether they are more advanced or just getting started.

Chapter 1: What is Forex Trading

The importance of the number

The average daily volume of currency trading exceeds $ 2 trillion per day. That's an impressive number, right? $ 2,000,000,000 - it's a lot of zeros, no matter how you cut them. To give you such a perspective, it's about 10 to 15 times the size of the daily trading volume on all the stock markets of the world together.

Forex trading terminology

As with most specialized areas, the Forex market comes with its own terminology that can be utterly undecipherable to the uninitiated. Before we discuss how to trade in Forex, let's get you acquainted with those words and phrases to help you navigate the information more easily.

Ask Price: This is the price that a seller is willing to accept for a trade on the market.

Spread: This is the difference between the bid and ask price and is where the broker makes their money. The more volatility in the market, the wider the spread is likely to be.

Exchange Rate: A familiar term for vacationers, this refers to the value of one currency in terms of another. For instance, how many Euros you would get for one Australian dollar.

Currency Pairs: The Forex market does not deal with individual currencies, but with pairs of them. For example, the U.S. dollar combined with the Canadian dollar. Some are much more widely traded than others.

Cross Currency: A trade in which neither currency is the U.S. dollar.

Cross Rate: A currency exchange rate between two currencies in which neither are the official currency of the country in which that rate is given. For instance, if an American publication quoted an exchange rate for the Canadian dollar and the Japanese   yen.

G7 and G20: These seven countries – the United States, Italy, Japan, France, Germany, Canada and the United Kingdom – are the countries with the most major economic developments and represent over two thirds of the world's wealth. Their currencies are stable, creating currency pairings that have high volume and volatility. The G20 includes these countries but also others including China, India, Argentina, Australia, South Africa, South Korea, Mexico, Saudi Arabia, Turkey, Brazil and the European Union. These together make up four fifths of the world's trade and 85 percent of the gross domestic product on the planet. These currencies are the ones you will   focus   on   as   a   trader.

Restricted Currencies: Some governments do not allow trading or speculation with their currencies. This can be because there is a limited availability, concern about the effect of speculation or a desire to control foreign investment.

Pip: This refers to the smallest possible increment by which a currency can move in price. Some currencies are quoted to four or five decimal places, so a pip refers to 0.0001 or 0.00001 of that pound, franc or Euro. Others are quoted only to two decimal places, so a pip is 0.01.

Volume: In Forex trading, this refers to the number of units being traded at one time. One currency may only have five or ten transactions taking place on it over the course of a day, while another may have thousands upon thousands. The former therefore has a   low   volume   of   trade,   while   the   latter   has   a   high   volume.

Volatility: This refers simply to how much change there is in the trading price of a currency over time. The most that price changes, the more volatile that currency is said to be.

Margin: If you don't have enough money to invest in a trade, you can get a secured loan from your broker to increase your capital. This is known as using margin. Doing so involves a great deal of risk as, if the trade is not successful, you will find yourself in significant   debt.

Margin call: This term refers to your broker requiring you to settle your account, usually when a trade reaches a certain level of risk.

Speculating

Although commercial and financial transactions on the money markets represent huge nominal amounts, they remain pale compared to values based on speculation. The vast majority of currency market volume is by far speculative - traders who buy and sell for short-term gains based on minute-to-minute, hour-to-hour, and day-to-day price fluctuations.

It is assessed that more than 90% of daily trading volume is derived from speculation (i.e., investment-based foreign exchange transactions or transactions represent less than 10% of the daily trading volume). The breadth and depth of the speculative market mean that the liquidity of the global currency market is unmatched among global financial markets.

What is trading Forex

Forex trading is a form of trade where traders buy and sell currencies. Traders forecast the value of one currency to another so that they can make a profit. The reason why they are traded in pairs is this. Unless you compare it with another currency, the value of one currency doesn't change.

In forex trading, you represent currency pairs as shown below:

EUR/USD

The base currency is the first currency while the quote currency is the second currency.

Why Forex trading?

There are many things that the Forex market has to offer. Some of them are listed below:

Accessibility. Ever wondered why the Forex market has the largest trading volume? It's because of the level of accessibility that Forex market presents. All that you need to participate in forex is a computer with a stable internet connection.

Narrow focus. The forex market has more than 8 major trading currencies. A small market means that there is little chance for confusion.

24-hour market. If there is anything that you can count on in the forex market, it is open 24 hours daily.

Liquidity. The major trading platform across the world is the forex market. High volumes of trade make it one of the best liquid market. This means that under normal market conditions, traders can still buy and sell currencies as they prefer.

Impossible to corner the market. Since it is the largest platform, it's not easy for one to deceive the market.

Trade opportunities

There are two trade opportunities in the Forex market.

Buy trade

The opportunity to buy trade is explained using the following scenario. Let's say that you think the current EURO value is growing strong against the US dollar, and you can opt to open a trade position to buy euros hoping that the currency value continues to be strong against the US dollar. In this case, the bearish currency is the US dollar while the bullish one is the euro.

Sell trade

On the other hand, if you have a strong belief that the euro should weaken against the US dollar, you may choose to open a trade position to sell Euros hoping that the value of the currency decreases. In the following scenario, the US dollar is bullish while the Euro is bearish.

Tip

The base currency is the only place where you have a choice whether to sell or buy. The quote currency is where the opposite is applied. Therefore, if you decide to buy the EUR/USD, you'll be selling US dollars and buying Euros. When you sell the EUR/USD, you'll be buying US dollars and selling the Euro.

If you are traveling to a foreign country and you decide to exchange currency, technically, you'll be buying the currency of the nation you are visiting and selling your currency.

Even when you think you are new to Forex, you must have traded Forex before, but you didn't realize it. For instance, if you travel to another country carrying your nation's currency, you are required to have your nation's currency to be exchanged to the currency of the country you are visiting. During the exchange, you will notice that the value of the two currencies is not equal. The value may be less or more.

Currency exchange is not only for travelers. Even the difference in price can be a motivation for you to trade. Across the world, thousands of financial transactions happen every hour. Many of these transactions involve organizations exchanging the value of one currency for another. With so many currency exchange rates taking place, the currency values are dynamic.

When compared to another, the value of one currency may be higher during the day because of economic and political news. This means that in the evening, currency may be weaker than another but then become stronger by midnight. These dynamic changes in the currency value are what cause Forex traders to make profit or loss in the Forex markets.

How to profit from Forex

You don't need to be a financial expert or genius to realize that the most prominent market attraction feature is the profit potential. First, let's make it clear that the Forex market is not a platform for millionaires alone. This platform also gives a chance to traders with little capital. There are specific forex brokers who allow one to trade with as little as $25.

What then is the chance of making a profit if one can start with this low investment? One thing that you should know is that you can use leverage to trade. When you trade with leverage, you can open positions worth $10,000 while you invest as little as $25.

Another important fact about the Forex market is that any movement causes the prices to change. In other words, traders have a chance to trade to make profit or loss.

While Forex trading can be highly profitable, it is also dangerous. Therefore, you should be aware of the risk, and don't make a mistake to risk money that you can't afford to lose.

Trade opportunities

There are two trade opportunities in the Forex market.

Buy trade

The opportunity to buy trade is explained using the following scenario. Let's say that you think the current EURO value is growing strong against the US dollar, and you can opt to open a trade position to buy euros hoping that the currency value continues to be strong against the US dollar. In this case, the bearish currency is the US dollar while the bullish one is the euro.

Sell trade

On the other hand, if you have a strong belief that the euro should weaken against the US dollar, you may choose to open a trade position to sell Euros hoping that the value of the currency decreases. In the following scenario, the US dollar is bullish while the Euro is bearish.

Tip

The base currency is the only place where you have a choice whether to sell or buy. The quote currency is where the opposite is applied. Therefore, if you decide to buy the EUR/USD, you'll be selling US dollars and buying Euros. When you sell the EUR/USD, you'll be buying US dollars and selling the Euro.

If you are traveling to a foreign country and you decide to exchange currency, technically, you'll be buying the currency of the nation you are visiting and selling your currency.

Even when you think you are new to Forex, you must have traded Forex before, but you didn't realize it. For instance, if you travel to another country carrying your nation's

12

currency, you are required to have your nation's currency to be exchanged to the currency of the country you are visiting. During the exchange, you will notice that the value of the two currencies is not equal. The value may be less or more.

Currency exchange is not only for travelers. Even the difference in price can be a motivation for you to trade. Across the world, thousands of financial transactions happen every hour. Many of these transactions involve organizations exchanging the value of one currency for another. With so many currency exchange rates taking place, the currency values are dynamic.

When compared to another, the value of one currency may be higher during the day because of economic and political news. This means that in the evening, currency may be weaker than another but then become stronger by midnight. These dynamic changes in the currency value are what cause Forex traders to make profit or loss in the Forex markets.

Forex is commonly known as foreign exchange or FX, and it involves the buying and selling of different currencies with the aim of making profits based on the changes in the value. The forex market is the largest market in the world; it is larger than the stock exchange market. Therefore, it attracts many traders. There is high liquidity in the foreign exchange market, and as such, this attracts both the experienced and the beginner traders. In fact, the forex trade market is so large that all the stock markets in the world cannot match its capacity. The foreign exchange market is decentralized across the globe; therefore, all the different currencies in the world are traded freely.

Chapter 2: Analyzing the Financial Market

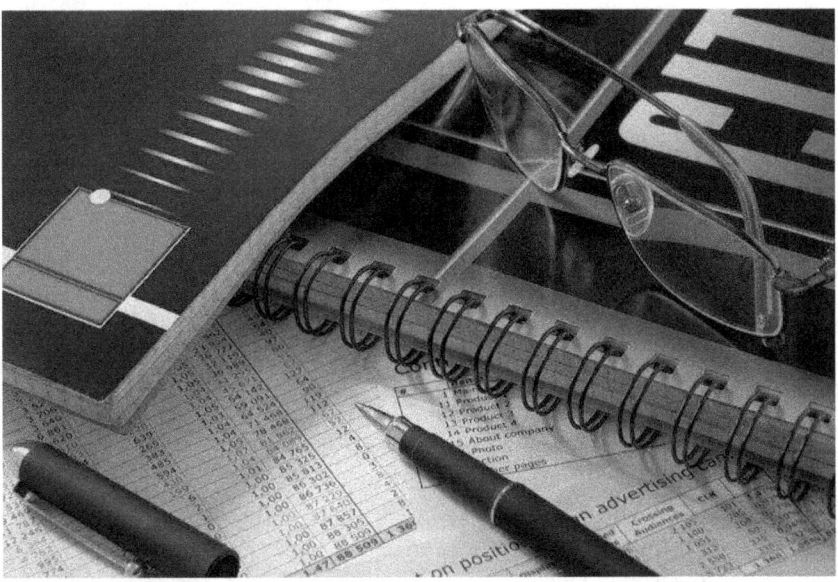

Fundamental analysis

Fundamental analysis is one of the most important elements which you need to take into consideration when assessing your deals. Without this type of tool, it will be very hard for you to assess a potential deal objectively.

Also, we will be looking at the elements that make up fundamental analysis. These individual elements will help you to process the information which is available to you throughout the various sources of data and analytics.

Fundamental analysis, like, technical analysis, are approaches which are based on statistical models and data. They are used to provide quantitative and objective information which can be used to support a trader's assessment of a deal. This allows for reasonable assumptions that can serve as a means of evaluation of potential deals.

The main use and purpose of fundamental analysis are to give traders and investors a clear understanding of the trends and patterns which comprise the reasoning behind a deal. Without it, the trader's sole reasoning for a deal would a subjective valuation of a deal in which it would be no more than just a gut feeling about what could happen. Needless to say, "gut feelings" can result in very flawed logic. Thus, not using the analytics tools out there will lead you to essentially make trades based on your own intuition.

While using your intuition is hardly irrational, especially if you are an experienced trader, having analytics tool which you can rely on, are an essential component to any successful trading strategy.

Definition of fundamental analysis

As stated earlier, fundamental analysis is a quantitative approach of key variables which can be used to make an assessment of market conditions. As such, fundamental analysis looks to take economic and financial information as the basis for the main assumptions supporting a FOREX trade.

While fundamental analysis and technical analysis can be used in any type of trading, the types of variables and information considered will vary from asset to asset. Consequently, the information used by stock traders will vary in comparison to the information used by FOREX traders. Therefore, there is a high degree of specialization in the type of information utilized by various types of traders.

At its core, fundamental analysis is about understanding where currency derives its value.

Earlier in this book, we defined what money is and what factors affect its value. As such, fundamental analysis is all about following the indicators which can provide investors clues as to where any given currency will trend.

Of course, there are structural issues in a country's economy which can undermine the value of its currency. But beyond that, it is mainly a question of understanding the macroeconomics supporting a currency.

Does that mean you have to become an economist to follow these trends?

Well, it helps if you are. But in reality, you don't really need to become an economist. Anyone can gain a keen understanding of the trends and behaviors supporting a currency. This is why part of your fundamental analysis tracking should be at least a casual following of countries' economic news.

For instance, if you hold US Dollars but decide to trade Pound Sterling and Euros, you might want to keep up with European news, publications by the ECB, and other analyses that can point toward the factors influencing the economies in Europe.

The methodology of fundamental analysis

The basic methodology of fundamental analysis is the comparison of economic indicators over a period of time. These indicators allow you to visualize the trends in the economy and perhaps determine what may or may not happen to that country's economy, and by extension, its economy.

Let's consider such variables regardless of the country under analysis: inflation.

In general, inflation is seen in the overall increase in prices. As such, inflation, or lack thereof, is seen across the board increase in price of all the commodities and products over a specific period of time. The most common timeframe for measuring inflation is monthly. However, there are also yearly measurements that are published.

Also, inflation can be the result of a currency's loss of value, specifically, its loss of purchasing power. Therefore, if a currency loses value over a period of time, it is not so much that products cost more to consumers, it is that the currency is able to purchase less.

Based on these two concepts, investors and the general public can track the price of a currency. If a country is being wracked by inflation, the currency will drop in price as compared to other, stronger currencies, especially if investors and the general public are looking to dump that currency and acquire a much "safer" currency.

The most common measure of inflation is the Consumer Price Index. Most countries calculate this variable by tracking the patterns in prices of a basket of goods as it would be nearly impossible to track the price of every good and service in an economy.

Consequently, the Consumer Price Index serves as a primary measure of what price levels are doing in an economy over a period of time, usually monthly or annually. In the United States, the Core Inflation indicator serves to provide information on the trends affecting the inflation of a country.

Another way in which inflation can be seen is through the calculation of the Purchasing Power. What this does is visualize how many goods and services can be purchased with the same amount of money over a period of time. This is measurement is not that obvious on a year to year basis. But when you visualize it over longer periods of time, say, 10 years or more, you can see some stark contrasts in the loss of purchasing power. However, when a currency is in serious trouble, these losses in purchasing power can be observed much more easily in a short period of time.

Why is inflation important?

Inflation is one of the most important factors when considering the value of a currency as rampant inflation can zap its value in a very short period of time. We have mentioned examples in the Turkish Lira, the Argentine Peso and Zimbabwe Dollar.

Perhaps the best example of what can happen when inflation gets out of hand is the Venezuelan Bolivar. Over the last couple of years, Venezuela has experienced hyperinflation. This is when inflation reaches over 50% in a period of 6 months. However, the International Monetary Fund estimated that inflation is Venezuela has touched over 1,000,000%. Yes, that's right, on million per cent.

In this case, the hyperinflation was not caused so much as a result of prices going up, but rather, an artificial devaluation of the currency due to irresponsible and reckless money printing. When governments take to the printing press in order to cover their budgetary deficits, especially when they can't collect more taxes or earn more revenues from exports, they might be tempted to just print more money.

Printing money creates an artificial excess of the money supply. Therefore, people now have much more currency than they did before. On the surface, that is positive for the people. But if the printing continues for an indefinitely, then it becomes a question of time before prices adjust to the new levels of currency in circulation.

In a nutshell, this is what happened to Venezuela. Once inflation began spiraling out of control, the Venezuelan government could do very little to restore confidence in its currency again. They had no choice but to revalue its currency. However, since Venezuela does not have a strong economy backed by anything else other than oil, its new, revalued currency quickly began losing value, as well.

If you were trading Venezuelan Bolivars on the FOREX market, you would have gotten hammered for one simple reason: your Bolivar position would have been worthless as no one else would have been interested in purchasing your Bolivars. Therefore, anyone who held Bolivars at one point needed to get out of them as fast as possible. Consequently, if you did not get out in time, you would have been stuck with very nice-looking pieces of paper which hold little value.

The above example serves to indicate how treacherous inflation can be. This underscores the fact that understanding the dynamics of technical analysis will allow you to think twice about trading currency that doesn't check off the right fundamentals. In addition, you need to be on the lookout for the right price dynamics. When these dynamics check out correctly, you can be sure that you will make the right deals based on solid fundamentals.

That is why doing your due diligence is an integral part of making ensuring that you won't be betting on a hunch. Rather, you can feel confident that your trades will have a good chance of making money. While nothing is ever a sure thing, you can at least reduce the likelihood of losing by a good margin.

Technical analysis

In order to ensure that your successful trade percentage only continues to increase as time goes on, you will likely eventually find it useful to branch out from using fundamental analysis exclusively to using technical analysis as well. While some traders consider the two types of analysis to be at odds with one another, the fact of the matter is that a balanced approach that uses each, when required, is always going to be the most effective in both the short and the long-term.

Technical analysis studies past market trends with the goal of accurately predicting those that are likely to occur again in the future. Technical analysis is ideal for those that like the idea of determining future performance by looking at previous prices, without having to dig through mountains of paperwork to find the details you are looking for. While the past will never be able to truly predict the future 100 percent of the time, technical analysis is useful when combined with a basic understanding of market mentality for generating predictions that are accurate within reason.

Price chartsA price chart is the primary tool of technical analysis. As the name implies, it charts the price of a given currency, on the x axis, as time passes, on the y axis. There are several different types of charts to choose from, but if you are just getting started with technical analysis then you will want to start with the line chart, the point and click chart, the candlestick chart and the bar chart.

Line charts: The most basic chart of them all is the line chart. It shows the closing price for the currency in question over a set period of time. The titular line is then formed one the day's grouping of closing prices has been determined and they are then connected with the purpose of determining a trend. While it doesn't include relevant details such as opening price or the results for the day overall, it will tell you if the day is positive or negative while also cutting out all of the noise that is so common in most other charts. As such, it can be an extremely enlightening place to start if you are looking at a new currency for the first time.

Bar chart: When compared to a line chart, a bar chart adds in the additional details related to a currency's movement throughout each day. The top and the bottom of the bar are going to represent the high and low for the day respectively and the closing price is denoted by a dash found on the right side of the bar. Meanwhile, the dash on the left side of the bar is going to show the starting price. Finally, if the overall value of the currency increased for the day then the bar will be black and if it decreased it will be either red or clear depending on your trading software.

Candlestick chart: A candlestick is similar to a bar chart in many ways, though it also provides additional relevant information that is more detailed overall. It includes the range for the day, expressed as a line, as with a bar graph, but when you view a candlestick chart you will also notice a wide bar near the vertical line which indicates the degree of difference the price experienced over a given period of time. If the price increases for the day, then the candlestick will not be shaded in and if the price decreased throughout the day then it will typically be shaded in red as well.

Point and figure chart: While the point and figure chart are used less frequently than some of the charts that have been previously discussed, the point and figure chart has been in constant use for more than 100 years and can still provide insight when used correctly. Specifically, this chart is used to determine how much a price is likely to move without taking timing or volume into account. This makes it a pure indicator of price, without any of the market noise that might otherwise be attached.

Range and trend

In order to ensure that you can properly profit from the use of technical analysis, it is crucial that you determine if it makes more sense for your trading style to focus on trading via trend or trading via range. While the two are both based on the price of the currency in question, they use that information quite differently in practice which means you are going to want to focus on either one or the other for the best results.

If you feel as though your personal trading style would benefit from making trades that mostly go with the flow, then you are going to be more interested in trading via trend as this will tell you what other traders are up to. Your goal in situations like this will be to determine which trends are most likely going to be the most robust in the near future, so you have the maximum amount of time to jump on them, reaping a lion's share of the profits in the process. If you are considering this type of trading, then you will want to stick with smaller trades as you can lose out if a trend fails to materialize in the expected way at the wrong time. Trading via trend is ideal for those who prefer high risk and the greater potential for reward it brings along with it.

Range trading, on the other hand, is better suited for those who are willing to forgo some amount of profit for more reliable returns. The range in question is going to be the price that a given currency is going to return to twice or more throughout the time you are holding it, allowing you to profit each time. The market is going to present you with different challenges every single day in the form of different trends and potential opportunities.

Regardless of this fact, the movement typically tends to operate in ways that seem completely random, though its true intentions can be found once you determine where to look. The opening range has been profitable for trading professionals for decades as a profitable way to start off with an idea of the market's mood to make any profits that are coming up even easier to obtain.

When you take advantage of the opening range for a starting point, you ill then be able to locate the truth of the current market to determine if the bulls or bears are going to be in charge at the moment. In order to get the most out of this practice, it is crucial that you understand the opening range for low and high levels as they are of critical importance when it comes to levels of resistance and support throughout the day.

Understanding these details will make it far easier for you to anticipate levels in the market that are more likely to reverse or increase the changes you are seeing. Looking at the trading day from this perspective is going to make it easier for you to make the right moves at the right time to allow you to determine when future movement is forthcoming, so you can be in the right place at the right time.

This doesn't mean you won't be able to act if you can't find the perfect entry point each and every time. All it means is that you will simply need to get in at a point where you will be in an ideal position for the next time the cycle repeats itself. You should also keep in mind that of the two strategies, range trading can take more resources to utilize properly which means you will want to have a substantial bankroll before you put it into effect.

Start off on the right foot

In order to use technical analysis effectively, you will need to understand that it functions around the idea that the price of a given currency is going to fluctuate in the future based on a number of identifiable patterns that can be seen in its past. As such, unlike with fundamental analysis where you might have trouble finding enough data to make a rational choice, with technical analysis you will have more data than you can ever hope to sort through. You will have plenty of tools to help you sort through all of this information, including things like trends, charts and indicators that will point you in the right direction.

While many of the technical analysis techniques might seem overly complicated at first, at their most basic they are all looking for different ways to determine trends that are going to form in the future along with the strength. Choosing the right trends at the right time is the first step to becoming a successful forex trader in the long-term.

Understand the market: Technical analysis is all about measuring the relative value of a particular trade or underlying asset by using available tools to find otherwise invisible patterns that, ideally, few other people have currently noticed. When it comes to using technical analysis properly you are going to always need to assume three things are true. First and foremost, the market ultimately discounts everything; second, trends will always be an adequate predictor of price and third, history is bound to repeat itself when given enough time to do so.

Technical analysis also believes that the price of a given underlying asset is ultimately the only metric that truly matters when it comes to understanding the current state of the market. This is the case because any and all other facets of the market have already been factored through to the price before it reached the point it is currently at which means that analyzing anything besides the price is, simply put, a waste of time.

Furthermore, technical analysis holds to the fact that the value of the underlying asset in question moves based on a trend that is well established which means it can be tracked as long as you know what it is that you are looking for. From there, it is really just a matter of time before the trend comes back around and you can take advantage of it once more. This is a viable strategy as it is more likely that an existing trend is going to reemerge than it is for a completely new trend to show up in its place.

After all, history is always going to repeat itself. This isn't just a saying, it is an unavoidable part of human nature, specifically, people like patterns. This means that if there is a pattern in a series of data, you can expect people to find it. Once it is found, you can then rest assured that they will do everything they can to take advantage of it. This will be the case each and every time the pattern is found which means that, if you find the pattern first, you can set yourself up to take advantage of it in the most effective way possible.

This is what allows many of the common technical patterns that are in use today to continue to be useful despite the fact that they have been in use for 100 years or more. This just goes to show that public opinion and action in relation to price changes is always going to be the same no matter what.

All about trend: Being aware of trend and how it can affect the ways you will analyze a specific trade is key to your long-term success through technical analysis. When on the lookout for trend, it can be any clear direction that the price of a given currency is taking that is clear enough to cut through all of the noise that naturally infects the market as a whole. Trends can be either strong enough to see from a mile away or weak enough to easily miss even if you are looking for them. Essentially it just means that just because a given trend isn't immediately visible then this doesn't mean it isn't there. Likewise, you are going to always want to ensure that the trend you think you are following is really there as it can be easy to misinterpret false data if you aren't careful.

The best way to ensure that the trend you are following is actually worth following is going to be to focus exclusively on the lows and highs and leave everything else out of the equation. This way you will be able to easily determine if the lows continue to increase (signaling an uptrend) or if the highs continue to decrease (signaling a reversal). You may also uncover a horizontal trend which shows that nothing much of

20

anything is happening at the moment and you might be better off waiting to get into the market until something more well-defined comes along.

Tapping into a specific long-lasting trend can allow you to assume that the net time it comes back around it is likely to be even more pronounced. You will want to keep an eye on things until the trend starts to materialize, however, just in case. If you find yourself watching a short trend, then you will need to expand your focus and ensure you aren't looking at a smaller part of a larger trend by mistake. The easiest way to do so is to simply choose a longer timeframe and see what there is to see.

While this will naturally make things more cumbersome, it can also make it far easier to catch a mistake that you may not otherwise be aware that you are making. The opposite can be true as well, if you are having trouble catching the right shorter trend, then a narrow focus across a shorter timeline might be just what the doctor ordered.

Trend mapping: After you have picked out the trend you are interested in finding more about, the next thing you will need to do is create a trendline that will let you map out all of the details as you come across them. This can be accomplished by simply drawing a straight line through the data points to make the trend more visible. If the trend is positive, then you will want to connect the dots of the various lows that are being measured while if it is a negative trend you will want to connect the relevant highs.

This line is what is known as the resistance line and it represents the market's natural inclination to push back once prices hit a point that is either significantly above or significantly below the average. This doesn't indicate the likelihood of the next price movement, just its overall limits. Once you have created the initial line, you will then want to create an additional pair of lines, one for the support level and one for the resistance level.

The support line will connect all of the lows while the resistance lines will connect all of the highs. The resulting channel that you then create will likely be either positive or negative though neutral channels representing sideways movement are also possible. Regardless, the channel you create needs to continue for a long enough time to show where the price breaks away from the status quo. This moment is going to represent your ideal entry point that will give you the best chance see the greatest overall return on your investment.

Currency forecasting

This section undersees the different models of currency forecasting used by analysts at large investment banks. There are seven main models of monetary forecasting: Currency Substitution model, Asset Market Model, Real interest rate differential model, Monetary model, Interest Rate Parity (IRP), Purchasing power parity (PPP), Balance of payments theory.

Currency Substitution model

The Currency Substitution model is a continuation of the monetary model because it takes into account the flow of investors from a country. It postulates that the transfer of private and public portfolios from one country to another can have a significant influence on exchange rates. The ability of people to change their assets in national and foreign currencies is called currency substitution. After adding this model to the monetary model, the evidence shows that changing expectations of a country's money supply can have a decisive impact on the country's exchange rates. Investors examine the money model data and conclude that a change in cash flow is about to occur, which changes the exchange rate and invests accordingly, making the money model self-sustaining and feasible. Investors who subscribe to this theory are only jumping the movement of the monetary substitution model towards the model currency party.

Asset Market Model

The standard premise of this theory is that the influx of funds to other financial assets of a country, such as stocks and bonds, increases the demand for the currency of that country (and vice versa). As evidence, the promoters point out that the amount of funds invested in investment products, such as stocks and bonds, now reduces the number of funds exchanged as a result of transactions in goods and services for export and import. The asset market theory is fundamentally the opposite of the balance of payments theory because it takes into account the capital account of a nation instead of its current account.

A dollar-based theory: Throughout 1999, many experts argued that the dollar would fall against the euro because of the US current account deficit and the overvalued Wall Street deficit. This was based on the logic that non-US investors would start withdrawing their US equity and bond funds in healthier markets, which would

22

weigh heavily on the dollar. However, such fears had persisted since the early 1980s, when the US current account reached a record level of 3.5% of GDP at the time.

Over the last two decades, the balance-of-payments approach to assessing the behavior of the dollar has given way to the asset market approach. This theory continues to influence specialists because of the enormity of the US capital markets. In May and June 2002, the dollar plunged more than 1,000 points against the yen as equity investors fled the US stock markets because of the accounting scandals that hit Wall Street. While the scandals were down at the end of 2002, the dollar rose 500 basis points from a low of 115.43 to $ 120.00 against the yen, although the current account balance remains unchanged all the time in deficit.

Real interest rate differential model

The theory of the real interest rate differential states that exchange rate movements are determined by the level of a country's interest rate. High-interest countries should have their currencies valued, while low-interest countries should see their currencies depreciated.

Basic Principles of the Model: Once a country has raised its interest rates, international investors will find that the return of the country's currency is more attractive and therefore buy the currency of that country. The figure below showed the validity of this theory in 2003 when interest rate spreads were close to their wider levels in recent years.

The data in this chart shows a mixed result. The Australian dollar had the highest base spread and also the highest yield of the US dollar, which seems to justify the model as investors bought the highest yielding Australian currency. The same is true for the New Zealand dollar, which also outperformed the US dollar and gained 27% against the US dollar. However, the model becomes less convincing when comparing the euro, which has gained 20% against the dollar (more than all currencies except the NZD), although its basic gap is only 100 points. The model is therefore seriously challenged when comparing the sterling yen and the sterling. The yen differential is -100 and appreciates by nearly 12% against the dollar. At the same time, sterling gained only 11% against the dollar, despite a huge differential in interest rates of 275 points.

This model also highlights the fact that the expected persistence of this change is one of the major factors in determining the severity of an exchange rate response to a change in interest rates. In simple terms, an interest rate increase that is expected to last five years will have a much greater impact on the exchange rate than if the increase were to last only one year.

Monetary model

The monetary model argues that exchange rates are determined by a country's monetary policy. Countries that follow a firm monetary policy over time generally have a valuation of currencies according to the monetary model. Countries with erratic monetary policies or excessively expansionary policies should see the value of their currency devalued.

23

How to use the money model. Several factors influence exchange rates in this theory:

• Provision of money from a nation.

• The expected future levels of a country's money supply.

• The rate of growth of the cash flow of a nation.

All of these factors are fundamental to understanding and detecting a monetary trend that may require a change in exchange rates. For example, the Japanese economy has been in recession and has been in recession for more than a decade. Lower interest rates are close to zero, and annual budget deficits keep the Japanese out of recession, leaving only one tool available to Japanese officials determined to revive their economy: print more money. By buying bonds and stocks, the Bank of Japan increases the country's money supply, which produces inflation, which forces the exchange rate to change.

It is in the area of excessive monetary policy that the monetary model is more successful. One of the few methods in which a country can prevent its currency from depreciating strongly is to conduct a restrictive monetary policy. For instance, during the Asian currency crisis, the Hong Kong dollar was attacked by speculators. The Hong Kong authorities raised interest rates to 300% to prevent the Hong Kong dollar from being pegged out of par with the US dollar. The tactic worked perfectly when speculators were acquitted by these high-interest rates. The downside was the danger of Hong Kong's economy entering a recession. But in the end, the footprint and the money model worked.

Interest Rate Parity (IRP)

The interest rate parity (IRP) theory states that if two different currencies have different interest rates, this difference will be reflected in the price or the discount against the forward exchange rate to avoid risk-free arbitrage.

For example, if US interest rates are 3% and Japanese interest rates are 1%, the US dollar should depreciate 2% against the Japanese yen to avoid risk-free arbitrage. This future exchange rate is reflected in the forward exchange rate quoted today. In our example, we say that the forward exchange rate of the dollar is not recommended because it buys less Japanese yen at the forward rate than in the spot rate. It is said that the yen is very expensive.

Interest rate parity has shown very little evidence of work in recent years. Often, currencies with higher interest rates increase because of the determination of central bankers to try to slow down a booming economy by raising rates, which has nothing to do with safe arbitrage.

Purchasing power parity (PPP)

The purchasing power parity (PPP) theory is based on the belief that non-exchange rates must be ascertained by the relative prices of a similar property base between two countries. Any change in the inflation rate of a nation must be counterbalanced by an

24

opposite change in the nation's exchange rate. Therefore, this theory shows that when a country's prices rise due to inflation, the country's exchange rate should depreciate to return to parity.

PPP basket of goods: The PPP basket of goods and services is a sample of all goods and services that are covered by gross domestic product (GDP). Includes consumer goods and services, government services, capital goods, and construction projects. Specifically, consumer items include footwear, food, beverages, tobacco, clothing, rental, water, gas, electricity, medical products and services, furniture, appliances, personal transportation equipment, fuel, transportation services, equipment hobbies , recreational and cultural services, telephone services, educational services, products and services for personal care and domestic operations, and repair and maintenance services.

Big Mac Index: One of the most common examples of PPP is the Economist's Big Mac index. The Big Mac PPA is the exchange rate that would leave the cost price of hamburgers in the United States as elsewhere, compared to real interest rate signals if the currency is undervalued or overvalued. For instance, in April 2002, the exchange rate between Canada and the United States was 1.57. In the United States, a Big Mac costs $ 2.49. In Canada, a Big Mac costs $ 3.33 in local Canadian dollars (CAD), which equates to only $ 2.12 in US dollars. As a result, the USD / CAD exchange rate is overvalued by 15% according to this theory and must be only 1.34.

OECD Purchasing Power Parity Index: A more acknowledged index was published by the Organization for Economic Co-operation and Development. As part of a joint OECD-Eurostat PPP program, the OECD and Eurostat share responsibility for calculating PPPs. The latest information on undervalued or overvalued currencies against the US dollar is available on the OECD website at www.oecd.org. The OECD publishes a table showing price levels for the major industrialized countries. Each column indicates the number of specified currency units required in each of the listed countries to purchase the same representative basket of consumer goods and services. In every case, the representative basket costs 100 units in the country whose currency is specified. The graph created then compares the PPP of a currency to the real exchange rate. The chart is updated every week to reflect the current exchange rate. It is also updated twice a year to reflect new PPP estimates. PPP estimates are derived from OECD studies; However, they should not be taken for granted. Different calculation methods will achieve different PPP rates.

According to OECD data for September 2002, the exchange rate between the United States and Canada was 1.58, while the United States / Canada price level was 122, which translates into an exchange rate of 1.22. Making use of this PPP model, the USD / CAD is once again overvalued (by more than 25%, which is not so far from the Big Mac Index).

Balance of payments theory

According to the balance of payments theory, exchange rates should be at their equilibrium level, that is, the rate that produces a fixed current account balance. Countries with trade deficits are seeing their foreign exchange reserves increase urgently because exporters to the country have to sell the country's currency to receive a payment. The cheaper currency makes the country's exports cheaper abroad, fueling exports and putting the currency in balance.

What does the balance of payments mean? Balance of payments account can be subdivided into two major parts: the current account and the capital account. The current account measures trade in tangible and visible items, such as cars and manufactured goods; the surplus or the deficit between exports and imports is called the trade balance. The capital account measures cash flows, such as equity investments or bonds.

Trade flows: A country's trade balance shows the net difference over a given period between a country's imports and exports. When a particular country exports less than it imports, the trade balance is negative or in deficit. If the country imports less than it exports, the trade balance is positive or in surplus. The trade balance shows the redistribution of wealth between countries and is an important means by which macroeconomic policies in one country can affect another.

Capital flows: There are also capital flows in addition to trade flows between countries. They record the inflows and outflows of a country, such as payments for entire companies (or for stocks), stocks, bonds, bank accounts, real estate and factories. Capital flows are affected by many factors, including the economic and financial climate of other countries. Capital flows can take the form of a portfolio or physical investments. In general, in under-developed countries, the composition of capital flows tends to be oriented towards foreign direct investment (FDI) and bank lending. For developed countries, because of strong equity and fixed income markets, equities and bonds appear to be more essential than bank loans and FDI.

Stock markets: Stock markets have a significant impact on exchange rate fluctuations, as they are an important venue for currency fluctuations in volume. Its importance is significant for the currencies of countries with developed capital markets, where inflows and outflows are important and where foreign investors are the main participants. The amount of foreign investment flows on equity markets depends on health in general and market growth, which reflects the well-being of specific companies and sectors. Currency movements occur when foreign investors transfer their money to a particular stock market. Thus, they convert their capital into national currency and increase demand, which allows the currency to appreciate. However, when stock markets go through recessions, foreign investors tend to flee, reconverting into their local currency and lowering the national currency.

Fixed Income (Bonds) Markets: The effect of fixed income markets on currencies is similar to that of stock markets and is a result of capital movements. The interest of the investor in the fixed income market depends on the specificities and the credit rating of the company, as well as the overall integrity of the economy and the country's interest rates. Foreign capital flows into and out of fixed income markets cause changes in foreign exchange demand and supply, which affect currency exchange rates.

Graphs, Charts, Candles

What exactly is the TradingView?

26

It is convenient charting software that also provides traders with the ability to network on the platform. TradingView is ideal for all kinds of trades, whether they are beginners or veterans. It is meant to provide you with a visual representation your trading (which is what we want after all) and supplements that view with tons of information about the trade.

Here are some of the cool features of the software:

Depending on how you would like to approach your trade, you can create simple charts or complex dynamic and multi-layered charts to track a plethora of markets. Additionally, if you feel like it, you can even create your own charts on the platform.

The software comes with different kinds of alerts that you can modify on the platform. Based on what kind of information you require urgent updates about, you can adjust up to 12 different notification settings.

For those who have honed their skills in charting software, TradingView also provides the feature of "Pine Script". What this script allows you to do is create your indicators and charts.

The platform also gives you access to over 50 exchanges around the world, enough to fulfill all your trading needs.

Finally, to add the cherry on the cake, TradingView provides a lot of educational materials. They have everything from videos to podcasts to articles giving you details on how you can trade and how you can manage finances, to how you should be looking at the various charts. Simply put, you have all the information you need to get started on the platform and become acclimated to the Forex world.

You can sign up for a free account, but it is not necessary to view some of the information on the platform. If you would like to simply make a quick reference, then head over to TradingView and you will spot a ticker on the top of the website giving you updates about the popular currency pairs.

MOBILE CHARTING PLATFORMS

Today's world is all about going mobile. If you have a business, it has become vital to target mobile users. It is for this reason that platforms such as Facebook, Google, YouTube, and Instagram all have special marketing campaigns that target mobile users.

In the same way, there are numerous mobile versions of charting platforms that you can access from anywhere in the world, as long as you are connected to a network.

But out of all the platforms available to you, which ones are actually worth looking into? Here are the ones you should consider if you are going to work on charts.

Netdania

One of the highlights of this app is that it provides you with trading strategies and ideas. The creators of the app have marketed the platform as a "personal trading assistant" and in many ways, it does function that way. For example, the app actually gives you a notification to let you know when the right time to go long or go short is. While doing this, it accumulates real-time news and economic information from around the world. Through social networking features, it shares strategies between various traders. This means that you can use the app to copy someone else's trading techniques if they have been successful.

As the app is connected to a cloud platform, you can easily share your info and details between multiple devices. Meaning that if you lose your mobile device, you can always download the app on another phone and get your data back.

Forex Time FXTM

What does Forex Time FXTM have in its favor that most other platforms do not? It has a degree of trustworthiness. After all, it has been used in nearly 180 countries and regulated in numerous regions as well. The platform is designed to work for both beginners, as the app itself is fairly easy to use, and for professionals, as it gives access to advanced features and educational materials. It also offers speedy functionalities and is able to make trades with just a percentage of a second difference between the time you execute and the time the order has been confirmed.

Trade Interceptor

Trade Interceptor is mainly made for advanced users. Though it does have a friendly interface and numerous educational materials to use, it is targeted to those who have more experience dealing with the Forex market. Its main charm is the fact that it provides access to a myriad of indicators that you can use for your trades. The app is also powered by the cloud network, allowing you to transfer your profile to any device. You can even play around with a trading simulator, designed to try out your strategies before you get down to working on real trades.

TD Ameritrade

TD Ameritrade makes a comeback! Earlier, we talked about the desktop version of the app. Here, we are going to focus on the mobile version. Not only is the app one of the most established and trusted platforms in the U.S., but it is also regulated (as we have seen before). The information on the app is presented in a clear manner. TD Ameritrade also focuses on other products such as futures, stocks, and options.

Chapter 3: Forex Trading Mechanics

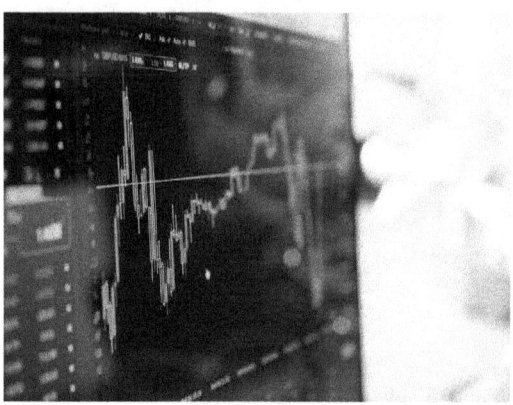

Buying and selling

The biggest mental barrier that newcomers face in currencies, especially those in many other markets, is that each transaction consists of a simultaneous purchase and sale. On the stock market, for example, if you buy 100 shares of Google, you have 100, and you expect to see the price increase. When you want to get out of this position, you are simply selling what you bought previously. Easy no?

Currencies in pairs

For most beginners, the most complicated aspect of Forex trading is not the volatility of the markets, but understanding how currency trading actually takes place and how to dip your oar into its waters.

The common mistake is to assume that it's a simple form of trading because it's top level – you're not dealing in what money can buy, you're dealing in the money itself. However, the market does not actually work with individual currencies.

Instead, it works with what are known as "currency pairs". While there are only around 180 currencies in the world, these can be paired in literally thousands of different ways because, as we're about to find out, it matters which order they are paired in and therefore whether you are dealing with GBP/USD or USD/GBP.

For instance, you might be working with the British pound and the U.S. dollar, a pair referred to as GBP/USD. You could be working with the New Zealand dollar and the U.S. dollar together, which would be referred to as NZD/USD.

Along with the pairings is the meaning associated with their order. It does, indeed, matter which currency is listed first in a pair and which is listed second.

The first currency listed in the pairing is the "base currency". It always represents a total of one and therefore is the stable base on which a trade is found. The base currency is used to figure out the answer to, "One of these equals X amount of that". In other words, if GBP is the base currency, one British pound is equal to X yen, X Canadian dollars and so on.

The second currency listed in the pairing is the "quote currency", and this is the one that alters to reflect the relationship between the two currencies in the pairing. The higher it is, the more of that second currency you will receive if you trade it with some of the base currency. For instance, if one GBP equals 1.4 USD, then for every British pound you trade you will receive $1.40 in American dollars.

This is where the jargon starts to get complicated. When you trade on the Forex market, you will either "bid" or "offer/ask".

To bid means that you are selling the base currency in the left side of the pairing in exchange for the quote currency on the right hand side of the pair. In other words, you are buying the base currency and selling the quote currency.

To offer/ask, you will buy the base currency on the left of the pair in exchange for selling the quote currency in the right hand side of the pair. In other words, you are selling the base currency and buying the quote currency.

It's absolutely crucial to memorize the difference between a bid and an ask, because what you'll get out of a trade depends entirely on the relationship between the two currencies. Get it the wrong way round and you'll make a loss where you thought you were making a profit.

You will also need to know that the Forex market specifically deals with how the value of the two currencies in a pair are changing. If the value of one is increasing, however, it doesn't necessarily mean that the other is decreasing. Though the two are paired in the trade, they are not solely going to be influenced by each other – you are simply removing two small cogs from the giant machine and holding them up against each other at a particular moment in time. What's happening in the rest of the machine (and, indeed, what's happening to that cog itself) is also going to influence its value.

The speed at which the two currencies are changing is also not always going to match. Just because the U.S. dollar is increasing fast in value doesn't mean the Canadian dollar is increasing at the same rate. This is where knowledge of the currency market comes into play. Simply looking at the pairing isn't going to tell you much about how it's going to look later in the day when certain markets close. You will need to look at the overall trend of the individual currencies to figure that out.

Obviously, the clearest trades are going to happen when one currency is weakening against the other, allowing you to buy or sell the weak currency at a great price. However, you can also make profit when both are strengthening, if they are doing so at different speeds.

Best currencies to trade

With forex, the basis of your trading currency will be the offered currency pairs of your dealer. However, since it is your first time to trade, you should stick with the eight major currencies.

Long and short

Going long

When you buy, you are looking for higher prices in order to sell at a higher price than what you purchase. When you decide to close a long position, you have to sell what you bought. If you shop at different price levels, you increase the lengths, and you get longer.

Getting short

A short, or simply a short position, refers to a position in the market in which you sold a stock you never owned. On the stock market, selling short stocks requires you to borrow stock (and pay a fee to the loan broker) before you can sell it. In the currency markets, this means that you have sold a currency pair, which means that you sold the base currency and bought the counter currency. You make so always an exchange, only in reverse order and according to the listing requirements of the currency pair. When you trade a currency pair, it's called a short sale or a short sale, and that means you're looking for the price of the pair to go down so you can buy it in a profitable way. If you sell at different price levels, you add shorts, and you shorten.

Chapter 4: Forex Trading mistakes

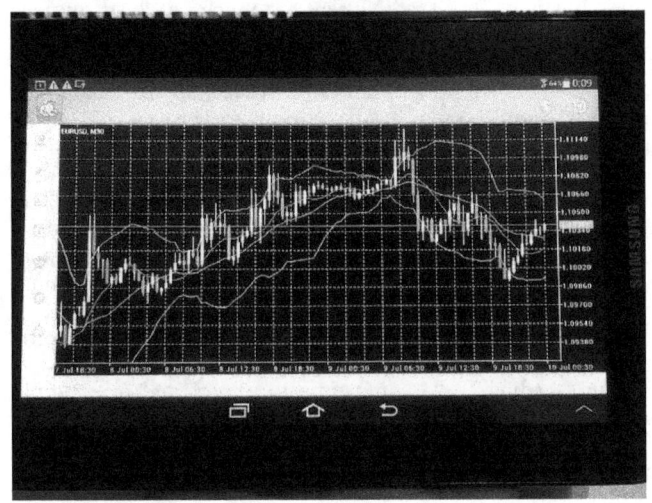

Most naïve traders who leave the market halfway make a lot of trading mistakes. Indeed, Forex is a profit making market, so even a tiny mistake can lead to severe failures. Hence, just like other markets in the financial industry, you must follow a few guidelines to trade Forex successfully. But, unfortunately, beginners don't have the patience to study the guidelines before entering the market. Anyway, I have concluded a list of common trading mistakes made by Forex traders. If you understand the mistakes, you'll be able to avoid making them in the future. As I mentioned earlier, Forex is all about self-learning. So, let's start!

Analysis paralysis

In the Forex market, there are so many opportunities as well as threats. As there are plenty of threats, you must prepare yourself to handle threats successfully. However, most Forex variables distract traders when they are trying to think straight about trading. If you want to find the right strategy, you must overcome all these problems. But, this can be tough for beginners. Anyway, you still have to find a good strategy to trade the market. So, even after finding a good strategy, how can a trader face the analysis-paralysis problem? Yes, it is still possible. Most naïve traders assume that they must look for more because more is considered better. But, in trading, more is never a good thing. Do you think that spending the whole day in front of the screen will help? Well, it will not help. In fact, it will lead to further confusion. You might come across numerous indicators, and it may give the idea that your current decision is false. And, that makes you emotionally weak, so this is when you fall into the problem of analysis-paralysis. The solution is to stay away from the market if you have entered into a trade. The more you watch the market, the more you get confused.

Overtrading

Most beginners don't get to go a long way in trading because they overtrade. This may sound like something simple, but it is not! Trading way too much will lead towards losses. And there is no counter argument on this. The interesting yet sad fact is that naïve traders make great profits in demo accounts, but when they trade live accounts, they trade terribly worse. But, you must understand why this kind of behavior is present in beginners. Basically, when a trader trades the demo account, he or she doesn't become emotional. The reason is that the trader knows the demo account isn't real and even the money is fake. But, remember, if you don't practice, you will not trade well in a live account. The underlying reason for overtrading is emotion. The traders get attached to the market emotionally, and they overtrade as if they will not end up blowing their account. You can actually control overtrading. But for that, you must have a defined plan that you adhere to. To be said simply, instead of trading you are gambling! Instead of trading like a reckless gambler, you must develop a calm and realistic approach to trade the market. Of course, if you have been overtrading for some time, it will be difficult to stop at once. But, for now, you must not trade the live account, instead consider demo trading. Take some time to understand overtrading and the effects of it. Once you understand, you will not make a mistake again.

Risk and money management

Another mistake made by Forex traders is not managing risk and money when trading the market. If you want to achieve success in trading, risk management is important. The simple definition of risk management is controlling the risk to the level that you can handle. The beginners often follow this denial concept. They deny the fact that they may lose any trade at any time. They believe all the ads and fabricated stories about quick money in trading. Hence, they don't give enough attention to risk and money management. Just think, how reasonable it is to risk more than the amount that you can handle losing? Sounds insane, right? But, this is one of the most common mistakes. A single trade can wipe your account completely if you don't control the risk. If you don't manage risks, you are going to lose everything. If you are dreaming about profits, it is a good sign because you are motivated to make profits. But, if you are dreaming ONLY about profits, then it is not a good sign. You must think about losses as well. You must find the risk ratio that you can afford to lose. Most professional traders and Forex mentors recommend 2% risk, but still, the decision is in your hand. You must decide the ratio that you are comfortable with.

Improper or no trading plan

Not having a plan or having an improper plan both fall into the same category. Having an improper plan is more like having no plan. So there is not much difference. This is also another mistake made by naïve traders. Most naïve traders assume that they can create a plan later but that later never comes. Besides, you must have a plan when you enter the Forex market because, without a plan, it is tough to enter into or exit a trade. A plan makes you stick to your goals. When you don't have a plan, you tend to make decisions emotionally. You will pick some random trading strategy, and you will use any approach to enter into a trade. Plus, you will exit a trade without considering any important factor. Thus, if you have a plan, you'll plan your trade execution. Before selecting a trading strategy, you'll shortlist some of the strategies. And you'll have an exit plan. Likewise, you'll be trading like a professional. Of course, even professionals must have a plan. But more than a professional, a naïve trader must have a plan to keep things organized. It is crucial to have a written plan that acts like a roadmap. Honestly, there are numerous benefits that you gain from trading with a plan. If you don't believe it, you can test it on a demo account. Typically, when you do something without a plan, your vision will be absurd. Thus, a plan keeps your vision clear. You will know when to exit a losing trade and when to extend a profitable trade. So, it is all about having an effective trading plan!

Trading or gambling

Trading and gambling are two different things. But, due to greed, the difference between trading and gambling have become something that is hard to define. Of course, beginners have the urge to enter into the market. But once they enter, they don't think about ethics and morals. Instead, they develop a gambling mindset. They start trading as if they have been practicing trading. Well, you must not enter the live trading account if you have not mastered your trading strategy, techniques, or approaches. The way to differentiate yourself from a gambler is to practice trading. You must start with a demo account. Remember, you must not trade the demo account for the sake of trading. Instead, you must trade it for a certain period until you become comfortable with Forex trading. But then, some traders will not have real emotions when trading the demo account. Hence, it can be tough to manage emotions while trading the demo account. So for this, you must try your best to keep your emotions real while trading the demo account. Only if you keep your emotions real will you be able to manage to live trade successfully.

Ignoring stop-loss

There can be times when you are confident about the profit targets. But, it is always better to focus on stop-loss placement. You already know that Forex is a volatile market where things can change in seconds. There can be certain events that will change the currency values in a short time. These events will have a huge impact on your trading decision. Hence, stop-loss will protect your account from facing losses. Thus, even if you are a professional trader, you must not ignore stop-loss placement.

Avoiding news releases

You must understand that news releases have a huge impact on the Forex market. Certain economic factors will create changes in the currency pairs. Thus, even if you are not a news trader, you must keep an eye on the news releases because it will affect the currency value. If you avoid news releases, you might make huge mistakes, so it is better to keep yourself updated about the news releases.

Increasing trading positions

Some naïve traders are overconfident, so they believe that their trading targets 100% profitable. So, even if their anticipation doesn't go in the right direction, they still believe that the trade is going in the right direction. And they simply add more positions with the hope of a price reversal. If you make this mistake, you'll be increasing the losses created. If it's an open position, you must never add more positions to it because it will become a chaotic situation. So, don't add more positions to trade if you are not experienced enough to understand it.

Currency correlations

Forex traders believe that they can earn more profits if they take more than one day trade. Of course, you can make good money, but on the other hand, losses will be doubled. When you trade multiple trades, you will also be dealing with currency correlation. When the currency correlations have a similar setup, both losses and profits can occur. If you are handling with currency correlation, you must remember that you are dealing with risks.

Revenge is not sweet

If you are a naïve trader, losses can be tough for you. But that doesn't mean professional traders are happy about losses. Even the professional traders don't prefer earning losses, but they don't take revenge from the market. On the other hand, naïve traders take revenge. The revenge trading will not do any good to you because you will end up facing losses. However, to avoid all these you must accept the fact that losses are possible in trading. You can't run away from losses. But, you can always limit losses. Hence, instead of revenging the market you can focus on improving your trading style.

Lack of knowledge

Actually, I should have added this mistake to the top of the list. When you don't have the Forex knowledge, you are likely to move towards losses and failures. To enter into profitable trades, you must keep improving your trading skills. If you aim to become a skilled trader, you must keep feeding Forex knowledge. Try to learn new trading techniques, methods, approaches, blogs, and educational books about Forex trading. You must only enter the Forex market after understanding the whole market. Most naïve traders don't make an effort to learn the market, so they lack the Forex knowledge. If you are assuming that trading strategy will help you to support trading, you've got it wrong!

Along with the trading strategy, you must have all the other important knowledge to trade Forex successfully. But remember, the knowledge that is not practiced is worthless. Hence, you must practice demo trading with the knowledge that you have acquired through learning.

Improper trading goals

I know, money is important. But if you begin your trading journey with the ONLY aim of making money, it will be the same reason why your journey will end. If you want to become a profitable trader, you must set proper trading goals. If you stop aiming for money alone, you will be able to improve your trading path as well as the account. When you run after money without thinking about anything else, you might break Forex rules and trade without a limit. Maybe you might earn a few good trades initially, but in the long run, you will not be able to create a successful trading path.

Selecting the wrong broker

Most naïve traders don't select the right broker because their complete attention is on making money. They don't think about the ways to make money. Only if you find a good Forex broker will you be able to manage your trading account successfully. Also, your success begins when you find a good trader and deposit your capital on the trading account. If your account isn't managed successfully, you will end up losing your money. Hence, you must allocate time to find the right broker. You can use the tips that I have mentioned already.

Not knowing the purpose

For some naïve traders, Forex trading is an entertainment. They find out about Forex trading in an ad, and they think it will fun to trade Forex. So they just enter into the Forex market. But, this is not the purpose of Forex trading. If you are entering the Forex market, it is important to know for what purpose you are entering the market. Your purpose will decide your level of commitment, attitude, and the goal. Thus, set your purpose wisely to make money from trading. You must be consistent in trading if you want to see yourself as a successful trader.

Being greedy

The beginners are usually greedy to make more money in trading. In fact, greed is the main factor that makes traders fall into traps. Most beginners enter the Forex market with the wrong intention, and they assume they can become rich quickly. When you become greedy, you will begin to chase unrealistic goals. Of course, you can set goals, but it should be realistic. Only if you set the right goals, you'll be able to overcome mistakes. So for that, you must avoid being greedy to make more money.

Not understanding Forex psychology

You must understand that Forex psychology has a lot to do with Forex trading. In fact, it is one of the major parts of trading. Some traders fail to trade the Forex market successfully because they don't understand Forex psychology. Most Forex mistakes can be avoided if traders understand Forex psychology. But, naïve traders don't even consider Forex psychology as a part of the trading journey. I'll be discussing more Forex psychology in following chapters so you'll understand better.

It is not easy to learn the mistakes and to correct them when you are trading Forex. But, you are lucky because you are warned about the mistake beforehand. So when you are trading, you'll not make most of these mistakes. Studying and learning the market will always be beneficial so you don't have to think that learning the mistakes is a waste of time. Let me tell you, even if you learn these mistakes over and over, you will still make certain mistakes. But, remember to correct them to become a noteworthy trader.

Chapter 5: Choosing Trading Style

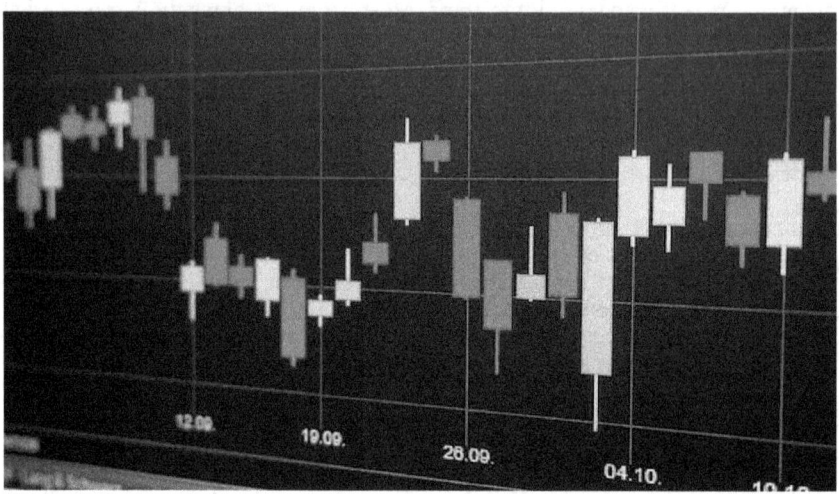

Short term

If you are more interested in shorter timeframes than what a carry trade can offer you, then the most important thing to remember is that you are going to want to prioritize trades that allow you to remain in control at all times, both when it comes to managing risk and sticking to the plan you come up with prior to starting. This will allow you to deal in charts that offer shorter time frames than many other forex investors. This doesn't mean that you will only want to stick to the short-term charts, however, as this will unnaturally curtail your profits in a way that will only lose you money in the long run.

To get started trading in the short term, the first thing that you will need to do is to find a pair of moving averages on the hourly chart. The trading platform that you use should have an option to automatically generate what you are looking for based on a predetermined time frame that you plug in. Once you have the indicators that you are looking for you will then be able to utilize them as a type of guidepost, allowing you to see how the market is moving in a time frame that will allow you to look before you act. If the resulting short moving average is less than the greater moving average, then you are going to want to lean heavily on a long position while if the opposite is true then you will need to lean on the short position in order to profit from the transaction.

Once you have found the trend that you are comfortable working with, the next is going to be to look more closely at the entries to match the direction of the trend you are looking into. Your main goal at this time should be to pick out the momentum that you have already seen on a longer chart as it is visualized on the shorter five or 15-minute charts. When taking advantage of this type of strategy, it is important to keep in mind that the timing is not always going to be in your favor when it comes to buying in. Instead, you are going to want to wait patiently for a profitable position to come along and the most reliable way to know when it arrives is to look for what is known as an exponential moving average.

When looking for this average you are going to want to keep an eye out for the trigger known as the eight-period exponential on the five-minute chart. Once this exponential starts moving in the direction of the overall trend, you will know that the strength of the trend and the speed at which it is acted upon are only going to increase. While this strategy may take a fair amount of micromanaging, it is well worth it for several reasons, starting with the fact that if you wait for the right trigger you know that other short-term traders are creating action based on the pair you are most interested in which means you can practically guarantee reliable profits for yourself if you jump in at a smart time.

This strategy is also a great choice when you are first getting started in forex trading, especially if your trading capital is rather limited. This is due to the fact that it allows savvy traders to move in on specific currency pairs early enough to get a great deal before the actual momentum picks up steam and the bullish price movement pushes the pair into prohibitively expensive territory.

This is also a useful strategy if you are looking to maximize the currencies you are looking to sell as it will provide you with the opportunity to know when a mass exodus on the currency in question is going to occur, allowing you to sell when the price is still high. It is still important to keep in mind that if a price sees a retracement in the short-term then the price is likely going to swing quickly but you will still wan tot double check what you are seeing to prevent a costly mistake.

To further maximize your profits using this strategy you are going to want to set your stop losses so that they are placed below the most recent high-water mark. That is, of course, unless you are currently heavily invested in a short position in which case you will want to set your stop losses in such a way that they are above the most recent low point of the currency to ensure that you don't suffer a loss if the trend losses strength earlier than you were expecting. This makes the short-term strategy extremely versatile as long as you are able to keep your emotions in check and set the right stops and stick with them as opposed to losing yourself in the moment in hopes of seeing things turn around.

This is not to say that working in the short-term is without risk, and the opposite is actually true in most cases. The short-term charts are far more likely to change with little to no notice than the long-term charts are, simply because any change that is noticed is going to be noticed first there. This means that if you hope to make money by using this strategy then you are going to want to do everything in your power to guarantee you are free to act with only a moment's notice. The best reaction in most situations is going to be waiting for the currency to return to a point of profitability before setting a new stop loss that is slightly in the money without getting greedy.

Long term macroeconomic trading

Long-term forex trading takes the nature of the basic buy and hold strategy. Here, you will not have to deal with a stressful environment. You can make as much time as you want to identify the best currency pair to invest in. Exiting the trade is also easy as you can wait as much as you want until you are satisfied with your profit. You can also care less about the day-to-day volatility that the forex market experiences and simply focus on your long-term vision. After all, it is very hard to predict to which direction the market is heading in just a short time as the effect of price-changing factors can have some delay. Long-term traders are also not required to make multiple trades every day. In fact, it is not uncommon to find long-term FX traders to only make less than 5 trades in a year. Unlike day traders who observe and analyze the market on a day-to-day basis, long-term traders are free to skip some days and not mind the market at all. Needless to say, being a long-term trader is much less stressful than a day trader. Long-term traders also have more time for themselves to do other things. They are not expected to be on the computer whenever the market is open. They can make a trade and come back to it whenever they want. Another notable advantage is that long-term traders usually enjoy the most profit per trade. Since the price of currencies fluctuates only slightly, it takes time to make a significant amount of profit. Last but not least, long-term trading has more chances to be able to recover from what otherwise would have been a bad trade. Take note that the price of currencies fluctuate continuously. Hence, just because it appears that a certain trade is at a loss, it does not mean that it will continue to be a losing trade. There is still a chance that it may recover and have you end up with a positive profit. For example, your worst trade today might just turn out to be the best trade after a few weeks.

Although it may seem that long-term trading is the better option, it cannot really be concluded that it is superior to day trading. After all, long-term trading also has its disadvantages. Long-term trading can easily get boring. If you are an active trader, the lack of action in long-term trading is not something that you will enjoy. You simply cannot wait for weeks and months just to know the outcome of a trade. Long-term trading is also vulnerable to so many elements including those that are unforeseen since so many things can happen over the course of a long-term trade. Hence, it is almost impossible to tell if your investment is really good enough or not as it may only be considered a good trade for a week but a bad investment the following week.

Scalping trading

If you would rather have small but consistent profit, then you should learn scalping. Since the potential profit is small, your risk will also be small. Of course, the key to profit with this strategy is having multiple small profits. Therefore, as a scalper, you need to be patient and diligent at the same time. If you are the type of trader who only wants to profit a big amount quickly, then this is not for you. Basically, scalping is where you enter a position and then leave it the moment that you realize a profit. Hence, this strategy is perfect for day traders. An important element of scalping is identifying the currency pair to invest in. Some traders merely rely on the volatility that is inherent in the forex market. However, it is worth noting that merely relying on volatility is not good enough. Instead, you need to rely on the hard facts and actual details. Therefore, as a trader, you are expected to do as much research as possible to help you develop your own understanding of the market.

When you use scalping, you should keep a close eye on the market while your position is open. All you need is a small profit, and then you should close your position. It is an excellent short-term strategy. Another important element of scalping is to know when to close your position. It can be very tempting to continuously hold a position, especially when you are profiting from it. However, keep in mind that holding on to a position for a longer time also increases your risk. After all, the fact remains that no matter how profitable a position may be, the market can still suddenly fall at any time. When you use scalping, you should minimize your risk as much as possible. Do not worry; if your position is truly profitable, you can still get back to it. The important thing about scalping is to be able to profit a little by risking also a little. Do not be greedy. Scalping is effective, but it takes time and you will have to do it many times to earn a significant amount of profit.

A notable disadvantage of using scalping is that it requires a large deposit; otherwise, the profit that you will get per successful trade would be almost negligible. If you do not invest a big amount, then you would earn very little even after ten successful trades using scalping.

Swing trading

Swing trading is a long-term trading strategy. As a swing trader, you should expect to experience multiple price fluctuations. This is norm on the forex market, especially if you hold a position for a long period. A good thing about being a swing trader is that you can earn a high amount of profit by the time that you close your position. Another advantage of using this strategy is that you do not have to study the market every day. Although it is still advised that you at least check on the market on a daily basis. This is just to ensure that your position is not being compromised. From time to time, you at see that you are losing the trade, but do not panic. Again, you should expect for some price fluctuations to take place. The important thing is to be in a profitable position when you exit the trade. Hence, do not allow yourself to be affected by the day-to-day volatility of the forex market for such is bound to happen.

Of course, you cannot expect to make a profit simply by holding on to a particular position for a long term. It is still important for you to choose the right currency to invest in. How you pick a currency depends on you. You may use financial analysis, technical analysis, or any other approach that you prefer. Unlike momentum trading where you normally just aim for a small profit, swing trading usually brings a significant amount of profit since it has a much longer trading period. The drawback is that this is also the style of trading that can lead to a serious loss since it involves holding your position for a long time. Although swing traders usually ignore the day-to-day fluctuations in price even in the case of a loss, these fluctuations can easily pile ofup over time and turn into a significant amount. This is also an excellent strategy to use for part-time traders as you do not have to follow the market regularly. Most swing traders only make a few trades in a month. The key is to focus on the quality of the trade than on quantity.

Pairs trade

Brokers have many different currency pairs. But the major four currency pairs used by traders include:

USD/JPY

USD/CHF

GBP/USD

EUR/USD

Which is the best Pair to trade?

If you are new, start with the major currency pairs because they have the lowest spreads. The EUR/USD is one of the best trading currency pairs.

How many pairs should you trade?

For new traders, you can start with one pair. Monitoring two or more pairs is hard. When you decide to trade with more than two, you will struggle to follow the price movements. To be safe, pick one pair, and stick with it.

Each pair has its properties. If you switch between currency pairs, you'll realize that.

Price action trading

Develop a trading plan

You now have the fundamental principles of Forex trading under your belt and you are aware what you are trading in and why. So how do you translate that into a practical application?

Every successful trader enters the marketplace with a clear plan in their mind and the reason they can then describe themselves as successful is because they follow it dutifully and religiously.

Now, while it's true that you can find software out there that will make those decisions for you, I strongly recommend that you avoid the temptation. Much as with those crash diets that never help lose more than a couple of pounds and the wonder medicines that do little else than taste unpleasant, those software programs tend to be snake oil. After all, if they really did work, everyone would be using them and everyone would be millionaires.

Instead, you're going to have to create your own plan and then rely on your hard work to research the markets, your intuition and your ability to assess risk to provide the rest.

To get started is relatively simple. You will need to provide yourself the answer to two questions:

What is the maximum loss you are prepared to make on a single position? (In percentage terms.)

What will be your stop loss position on your trades?

43

Every trader needs to know the answer to those questions, although everything else is fluid and personal. Your ability to analyze the market, the time of day you trade, your capital and risk ability – these things are all distinctly personal, which means there is no possible way to develop a plan that works for absolutely everybody.

Not to mention that the same strategy won't necessarily work in every market and on every trade or with every currency pair. You will need to develop a fluid mindset that can adapt your plan accordingly to the realities of the market.

So, with that in mind, how do you develop your personal strategy? Start with the two questions above, as these are designed to make sure that the capital in your trading account remains intact. Answer those questions with a mind to your trading account and to how much you can afford to lose before you no longer have the capital to continue trading. Your answers are the only ones to which you must adhere religiously, come what may. Consider your capital to be your prize possession and worthy of protection at all times.

A quick example to show you how those questions then apply to an actual trade. Let's assume that you've decided that your maximum risk on a trade is going to be $45, which equates to 2 percent of your capital (I would recommend never going above 5 percent), and that you've decided your stop loss position will represent three times the average pip movement of that currency pair.

Now let's assume you're looking at a trade that moves on average five pips within your chosen timeframe. You would therefore have a stop loss position of 15 pips. If you divide the maximum loss you're prepared to make by the number of pips, you get the number 3, which translates to $3 per pip.

So what does that mean? It means that you want a contract that balances out at $3 per pip.

You can, of course, then play with your equation. For example, if you enter into a contract with less risk than you're prepared to take, you can then increase your position later if your predictions bear out, adding more contracts until you reach that $45 maximum. Don't forget that the answer to these questions represents the maximum risk you're prepared to take, so you don't actually have to meet those numbers exactly as long as you don't exceed them.

Chapter 6: Forex trading strategies

Real time Forex charting

Swing trading is a trading style preferred by many retail traders because firstly, they contain entry and exit strategies that do not require one to keep checking the charts every few minutes or hours and secondly, it is a long-term strategy. The trading style is well suited for people with busy lives or even full-time jobs, therefore, cannot afford to watch the charts every other minute.

Traders that use the swing trading technique may use timeframes on the charts from as low as 5 minutes to an hour. Swing traders may combine both the fundamental and technical analysis to draw conclusions and make decisions. To a certain extent, it does not matter whether the market has a long-term trend and/or that the market is range bound because the forex swing trader will not hold the positions long enough for these factors to count.

However, volatility makes significant differences for swing traders because highly volatile markets suit them best. The higher the volatility, the higher the number of movements in the short term. As such, the trader has many opportunities to place his/her trade. Swing trading has a number of benefits including benefits from liquidity, sufficient volatility to create trade opportunities and relatively short time frames to make earnings.

Some traders find the extremely short-term trades exhausting because of the amount of time spent monitoring. They also find long term trading too boring and not active enough with too much demand for patience. As such, they settle for swing trading because it is simpler to use and has friendly time frames. Beginners also prefer this type of trading and try it out with demo accounts before getting into the real business.

In swing trading forex, certain techniques and strategies work well together to get the trader a win. Remember that swing trading is not just a trading style but also a strategy. Within this style, there are different strategies that a trader can use to swing trade safely. Keep in mind that swing trade operates over medium and short timeframes; that is between the day trading which requires a very short timeframe and the positioning trading which requires a very long term. The thing is, swing trading is short enough to create plenty of opportunities for traders but not so short that the trader has to stay glued to the charts. The following strategies are not strictly for swing trading, unlike other technical strategies.

The main concepts behind swing trade strategies are resistance and support. These concepts allow one to choose between two decisions; either follow the trend or go against the trend. The counter-trend strategies seek to make profits when the levels of resistance and support hold up. On the other hand, trend following strategies identify periods where the levels of resistance and support break down. In both cases, it is important that a trader can recognize a price action visually. Remember that markets do not follow a straight line. Even when the markets are trending ultimately, they tend to move in step like movements of up and down. When the market sets a higher high, traders recognize an uptrend, and when the market sets a lower low, then the traders recognize a downtrend. As such, most of the swing trade strategies seek to catch and follow a short-term trend. In other words, a swing trader will be looking for a trend, then he/she will wait for a countertrend, and after the trend has played out, he/she enters the market.

Automated Forex trading

Technology advancements have made it easy for forex traders to trade with utmost ease. The trade has adapted well to automated trading strategies, and with some training, a trader can reap the benefits of the available moves. A trader can set up programming entry, automated trades, limit prices and stop loss before he/she even makes a trade. The trader may also instruct the trading platform to transact when there are certain price movements or market conditions.

When a trader identifies a well revised automated strategy, he/she may have the chance to take advantage of the daily swings in the market without having to put all their efforts in keeping up with the movements in the market.

Calculating interest

A trader may have a hard time working with different currencies expressed as pips especially if they do not understand the pip valuation system. In forex, a pip is the smallest trade unit for every currency pair.

A typical pip calculator may also show the value of a pip for a particular pair based on a mini lot, micro lot, or standard lot. To use the calculator, one simply needs to enter the position details that include the currency pair, the trade size, the amount of money in the account, the position size parameters and the leverage. The calculator works out the value of the pip for each position in the chosen currency. The tool is very useful for the trader to keep track of the value of a position in the account.

Analysis based trading strategies

Learning how to trade in the forex market can be hard because of the numerous strategies available for the traders. As traders look for ways to maximize profits and minimize losses, they tend to change between the strategies. Sometimes, they do it so quickly that they will not learn any meaningful aspects of any strategy. The first stages of forex trading have certain technicalities, and as the trader looks to join the real trade after practicing with a demo account, he/she faces the challenge of picking an appropriate trade strategy. The strategies are so unique that people practicing a similar one would end up with different results. Despite the universal nature of the strategies, people will interpret the charts and indicators differently.

In order to avoid changing the strategy every now and then a trader should;

- Identify a strategy that is suitable for the timeframe he/she selects. A trader should pick a trading strategy that best resonates with their idea of profitability and success in the forex trade.
- Stick to a strategy for at least 6 months. The best way to choose a strategy that one can stick with for long it is doing a lot of up-front research. When one finds a strategy that is good for their expectations, then they may take it. One has to give him/herself time to learn how the strategy works.
- Understand that not all the things in the strategy are relevant for the trade. Learn as much as you can but do not cram every detail. There is too much information and memorizing all of it will result in a misunderstanding.

Trading style based strategies

Real-world and lifestyle considerations

Before you begin to identify the style and approach to trading that's right for you, think carefully about the resources you have to support your trading. As in most of the efforts of life , when it comes to trading on the financial market, there are two main features that people seem never enough: time and money. Deciding how much each one you can spend on currency trading helps to establish how you are pursuing your trading goals.

If you are a full-time trader, you have a lot of time to devote to market analysis and trading in the market. But as currencies are traded nonstop, you must always know which trading session you are trading in and the daily peaks and valleys of activity and liquidity. (See Chapter 1 for specific session details.) Just because the market is always open does not mean it's always a perfect time to trade.

If you own a full-time job, your boss may not like to take the time to follow charts or economic data reports while you are at work. This implies that you will have to use your free time to do your market research. Be realistic in thinking about how much time you can regularly spend, taking into account family obligations and other personal circumstances.

As far as money is concerned, we can not emphasize enough that commercial capital must be venture capital, and you should never risk money that you can not afford to lose. The default definition of **venture capital** is money that, if lost, will not

47

significantly affect your standard of living. Needless to say, borrowed money is not ventured capital - you should never use borrowed money for speculative transactions.

By determining the amount of venture capital you have for trading, you'll have a better idea of the size of the account you can trade and the size of the position you can manage. Most online trading platforms usually offer generous leverage ratios that let you control a larger position with less margin required. But it's not because they offer high leverage that you need to use it fully.

Short-term, high-frequency day trading

Short-term forex trading usually involves maintaining a position for a few seconds or minutes and rarely more than an hour. But the time factor is not the defining quality of short-term currency trading. Instead, pip fluctuations are important. Traders who follow a short-term trading style seek to profit by opening and closing positions multiple times after winning only a few pips, often as little as 1 or 2 pips.

When it comes to discipline, stockbrokers must be absolutely cruel when they make profits and losses. If you only wish to make a few pips in each trade, you can not lose much more than a few pips in each trade.

Working on the market requires an intuitive understanding of the market. (Some practitioners call this **rhythm trading.**) Money changers do not care much about fundamentals. If you ask a scalper for his opinion on a specific currency pair, she is likely to respond to the "Looks **Bid** " or "Looks **Offered** " lines (that is, she feels buying or underlying sales in the market - but at that time). If you ask again a few minutes later, she can answer in the opposite direction.

Successful stockbrokers have absolutely no loyalty to one position. They would not care less if the currency pair went up or down. They are strictly focused on next glitches. Their position works for them, or they come out faster than you can blink.

Here are some other essential guidelines to bear in mind when following a short-term trading strategy:

Concentrate your trading on one pair at a time. If you plan to capture price movements from second to second or minute to minute, you need to focus fully on one pair at a time. This will also improve your perception of the pair if this pair is everything you look at.

You have predefined your default trading size, so you do not have to specify it in each transaction.

Find a brokerage firm that offers clicks and transactions, so you do not experience delays or foreclosures.

Modify your risk and reward expectations to reflect the trading spread of the currency pair you are trading. With spreads of 2 to 5 pip on most major pairs, you will likely need to capture 3 to 10 pip per transaction to make up for losses if the market moves against you.

Avoid trading around dice throwing. Taking a short-term position in a data publication is very risky because prices can skyrocket after launch, throwing a short-term strategy out of the water. Markets are also subject to rapid price adjustments between 15 and 30 minutes prior to the release of key data when closing orders are triggered. This can result in a rapid change of position, which may not be resolved before the data is released.

Making time for market analysis

Calculating the amount of data and news that flows through the forex market on a daily basis can be really overwhelming. So, how can a trader track all the data and news?

The key is to develop an effective daily market analysis routine. Through the internet and online currency brokers, independent traders can access a variety of information.

We do not know many currency traders who do not follow any form of technical analysis in their trading. Even stereotypical marketers who practice anything are probably aware of the technical price levels identified by others. If you are a trader active in other financial markets, you have probably done a technical analysis or at least heard about it.

Technical analysis can provide insights into the path of major price changes, allowing traders to predict the scope and direction of future price changes more accurately. More importantly, technical analysis is the key to building a well-defined trading strategy. For instance, your fundamental analysis, data expectations, or simple instinct may lead you to conclude that the USD / JPY is down. But where exactly do you fail? Where do you make profits, and where do you reduce your losses? You can use technical analysis to refine the points of entry and exit of trading and decide if and where to add positions or reduce them.

Sometimes foreign markets seem to be more due to fundamental factors such as current economic data and comments from a central bank official. At that time, the foundations provide the catalysts for breaks and technical reversals. At other times, technical growth seems to be leading the charge - an interruption in trend line support can trigger long-term stop-loss sales and incorporate system models that are sold according to the interruption of support. Later economic reports may be against directional theft, but the data must be damaged - the media is finished, and the market is selling.

The market approach with a mix of fundamental and technical analysis increases your chances of detecting business opportunities and managing your business more effectively. You will also be better prepared to deal with markets that react alternatively to key technical developments or a combination of both.

Medium-term directional trading

As with short-term trading, the main distinction of medium-term trading is not the opening time of the position, but the number of pips you seek / risk.

When short-term traders seek to take advantage of the routine noise of small price movements, almost disregarding the general direction of the market, medium-term transactions seek to gain the right direction and benefit from more favorable exchange rate movements. important.

Almost as many currency investors fall into the medium-term category (sometimes called **momentum trading** and **swing trading**) as in the short-term category. Medium-term trading needs many of the same skills as short-term trading, particularly with respect to entry / exit positions, but it also requires a broader perspective, a greater analysis effort, and a lot more patience.

Capturing intraday price movements for maximum effect

The benefit of medium-term trading is to determine where a currency pair is likely to move in the next hours or days and developing a trading strategy to exploit that vision. Medium-term traders usually follow one of the following general approaches, with plenty of room to combine strategies:

Trading a View: Have a basic opinion about how a currency pair will likely evolve. The display operations are generally based on prevailing market themes, such as interest rate expectations or economic growth trends. Display traders must always be aware of technical levels as part of a global trading plan.

Trading the technical: Base your market perspective on graphical models, trend lines, support and resistance levels, and momentum studies. Technical traders usually identify a trading opportunity in their charts, but they must always be aware of key events because they are the catalyst for many technical breaks.

Trading Events and Data: Base your positions on the results of expected events, such as a rate decision from the central bank or a G7 meeting or individual data reports. Event / data traders usually open positions well in advance and close them when the result is known.

Trading with the flow: Trading based on the general direction of the market (trend) or on the main purchases and sales (flows). To trade with feed information, look for a broker that offers feedback on the market flow. Flow traders tend to be excluded from limited markets at short-term intervals and only enter when market movement is underway.

Different strokes for different folks

Once you have thought about the time and resources you can devote to currency trading and the approach you favor (technical, fundamental, or mixed), the next step is to choose the trading style that you want. is best. corresponds to these choices

In the following segments, we detail the three main trading styles and what they really mean for individual traders. Our goal here is not to advocate a particular trading style because styles often overlap, and you can adopt different styles for different business opportunities or different market conditions. Instead, our goal is to give an idea of the different approaches used by forex traders so that you can fully understand the basis of each style.

Order types trading strategies

There are different orders that you can give to your broker as to how you want to trade currencies. These orders may be used to control how you enter and exit the FX market. Hence, they play an important element in building a successful career as a foreign currency trader.

Market order

A market order is the most common type of order in forex. This order tells the broker to buy or sell a currency pair at the best possible price. This happens instantly and is always executed by the broker. A market order is the best way to enter the market as quickly as possible.

Entry order

As the name implies, an entry order is a way to enter the market. It is difficult to spend the whole day monitoring the market just to see when you will enter it. In this case, you can just use an entry order and be able to spend your time away from the computer. In an entry order, you get to enter the market once the price reaches a certain point.

Limit order

A limit order is often used to exit a market at a profit. This order directs your broker to buy or sell a specific number of units of a currency pair at a defined value. If you have a long position, then the limit order should be higher than the current market price. If you are taking a short position, then the limit order would be lower than the market price. This of it as a limiting line where you trade will be automatically closed once it reaches that line. Of course, once this line is reached, then you will receive whatever profit you may have into your account balance.

Stop order

A stop order is used to exit a trade. The purpose of this order is to control or limit the possible losses that you may experience. Hence, it closes a trade that reaches a certain level of loss. Although a stop order is not a good sign when its defined limit is reached, it is able to limit your losses and closes a trade in order to prevent you from losing more.

Stop loss orders

Risk control is very important in trading currencies. You need to decide how much you are going to risk per trade before you enter it. Stop loss order will automatically close your open trade at a predefined level and help you to prevent further losses.

Take profit orders

Take profit order will close your trade at a predefined level if price goes in the direction you anticipated. When that level is reached, your trade will be automatically closed.

Trailing stop order

Trailing stop order is order that let's your position move together with the price. It works both as **stop loss** and a **take profit** order. If you have a certain number of pips of profit you can trail your stop as price continues to move in your anticipated direction. If price moves by a certain number of pips against you (you define how many) your position is automatically closed.

Chapter 7: Psychology for trading

Be patient

Many folks who start out investing, regardless of the type of investment they choose, don't exercise patience. They tend to get caught up in the illusion that they could make hundreds, if not thousands, per trade.

Unrealistic expectations can lead individuals to think and believe that they can dramatically change their financial position in a matter of weeks. Sure, that is possible, but perhaps not in the way that you believe.

One of the most important characteristics of FOREX is that you do not need to start out with thousands of Dollars. In fact, you can start out with $200 or $300 and watch your seed capital grow. This is exactly where things get complicated. You can start off with such a low amount of capital, but in order to make it grow, you need to have patience. Starting off with $500 is not going to yield thousands and thousands of Dollars in profits.

This is just a question of pure mathematics.

If you had the opportunity to start off with thousands of Dollars, then you could conceivably make much more. But then again, the golden rule will give you the discipline moving forward to avoid making huge bets and risking your entire seed capital.

That means that if you really wanted to make a lot of money, then you would need to make multiple deals in order to make the returns which you might be expecting.

Thus, FOREX investing is just like trading stocks. You must be patient. You cannot expect to hit a home run on your first turn. But, if you do exercise patience, then you can find that sweet spot which will enable you to make the types of returns that you wish to achieve.

A realistic return of 6% to 8% is well within your reach. The most important thing to keep in mind is that earning these types of returns take skill. Developing such a skill is the product of learning and practice. Hence, the more experience you attain in FOREX trading, the better returns you will achieve.

Here are a couple of tips which can help you keep focus:

Start off with daily charts. Perhaps the easiest way of becoming proficient as FOREX trading is by using daily charts as a guide. Sure, there are hourly and even minute by minute charts. However, daily charts help investors become wise as to the potential of trades. So, daily charts are certainly a great way to get off to a good start. Bear in that you do not need to trade every day in order to make good returns from FOREX. This makes FOREX ideal for those who have a day job, or perhaps would like to combine it with another type of day trading endeavor.

Quality versus quantity. I am well aware that you understand the notion that a higher trade volume will increase your chances of earning a higher return. However, you have to visualize just what kinds of trades you are making. Are you making quality trades? This is something to keep in mind as poor-quality trades can lead you to lose money. Therefore, no matter the volume of trading that you keep up, you will end up making a lower return. My advice is to pull the trigger on those deals which you know will give you the best possible yields. This might mean that you'll end up spending a couple of days observing the action. But in this case, it's best to get into the action only when you are sure that you are making a good deal.

Think of trades as a limited commodity. When you think of your trades as a limited commodity, then you begin to imagine that you have a certain number of "bullets". If you run through them quickly, then you'll be out of ammo. In FOREX, you can quickly run out of ammo. And once you are out, you can only come back in with more ammo, that is, money. The last thing that you want to do is trade for the sake of trading. In addition, being emotional about your trades will only increase the likelihood of you making mistakes and losing money. As such, keeping your emotions in check is perhaps the single-most important thing which you can go to set yourself up for success. In the end, keeping your mindset neutral and focused on the prize will help you make successful deals most of the time.

Consequently, exercising patience will build a discipline inside of you that will help you become successful most of the time. If you choose to make patience an integral part of your trading strategy, I assure you that you will find FOREX trading to be a profitable endeavor.

Be disciplined

Since you must continue to execute trading signals during periods of loss, discipline is difficult. This must continue until you get a home run, even when the market is fooling you and taking your money.

Focus on maintaining business discipline and good money management practices. Do not change your business plan, no matter what the market does. Fine tune your plan if necessary, but only do so when your trading positions are closed to prevent them from influencing your plan.

The basic idea here is to examine speculative activities in the foreign exchange market as a business. Certainly, you will win in some transactions, and you will lose in some transactions, so consider this as part of the trading process. In general, you should always look to manage your business and your brokerage funds to stay in the game in the long run.

Trust the process

You trust the process by having the right attitude towards achieving your goal in Forex trading. The right attitude will always be able to suit your needs when you are trading in Forex. Having the right mindset and the right goals for your trades is something that will set you apart from others who do not know what they are doing or who want to be able to try different things without taking into account all of the problems that can come with trades that they are doing.

Having a new trader attitude while you are doing bolly band bounce trading is one of the best things that you can do. It is something that seems like it was perfectly optimized for people who want to be able to get the true best experience out of trading, and it is something that is great for beginners.

When it comes to bolly band bounce trades, you do not really need a specific attitude to make it work the best way possible for you. That is one of the many reasons why it is good for beginners and a reason why most people who are just getting started should choose bolly band bounce trading.

If you are working through the different processes of trading and you keep that same beginner attitude for trading, you **will** have problems that you will have to deal with because of the things that are included with the different options that you have. Always make sure that you are doing your best and that you are learning the right attitude.

It doesn't matter as much with bolly band bounce, but you will see major problems if you do the same thing with other Forex trade strategies.

Daily routine

Habits are the secret to success or failure in every endeavor. From childhood to adulthood, we are products of many different factors, including habits. As traders, we can only develop the right habits by establishing routines. Just like good behavior, we have to model proper trading habits which over time, become part of us. Forming habits can be hard work because sometimes, they can even take years. To develop these habits, it is essential to remain positive and consciously make these choices deliberately. Routine is the secret of most creative and gifted people as normally, they follow these routines like clockwork. Eventually, what happens is that routine soon becomes a habit and afterward bears fruits of consistency and success.

Is there power in a routine?

In trading, you can only make it with a routine. This routine should include, among other things, a trading plan. Routines vary widely, but there are some general aspects that transverse borders and professions. Below is an example of the elements that are likely to be found in the routine of a serious trader:

Ideally, the trader gets 8 hours of sleep a day.

Eat a healthy breakfast.

Identify the daily chart trend. This step is not as easy as the first two, and this is where the discipline starts. The daily chart trends are checked for the markets that are traded.

Identify key resistance and horizontal support levels at the start of the week.

Checking charts to scan for price action signals that have confluence with the resistance or chart trends.

Scanning for price action signals that may have formed in favorite markets after the New York Close

Setting up trades that have met the trading criteria and walking away until the next day

Checking open trades in the morning and taking note of what happened without taking any extra actions. It takes discipline to observe only.

This routine is short and simple. However, it is vital to realize that it does not say anything about consistently entering trades and analyzing the market. Instead, the trader approaches the market from a certain angle and at almost the same time daily. The mid is, therefore, inclined to turn this simplistic routine into a positive routine. You should customize your routine so that it fits within the confines of your life.

Why routines are powerful

While it is quite evident that routines work to your benefit, it does not hurt to get a scientific perspective on the same.

Routine is a game-changer because it affects creativity positively. Routine projects and gets through to the subconscious mind. Knowing how essential the subconscious mind can be in helping achieve better decisions, you can understand why routine is essential. Additionally, as you continue to do something every day and as part of your routine, you become better at it, and you start achieving better results than you would with active thought. The magic of success is in daily practice. A routine will keep you connected to the most important things in your day and helps you do things naturally, and that keeps you sane as a trader. Routines also help give you the best chance at synchronizing with the market, understanding its rules and synchronizing with it when you finally put a trading plan in place.

This method of trade works to your advantage in many ways. For example, it simplifies what is commonly a great and complex process of trading and also improves your trading results. These improvements in process efficiency and trade results happen in multiple ways:

By reducing the number of variables and amount of time needed to trade. This naturally corrects the trading mindset as you are not watching charts all day.

When you do not watch charts all day, you do not overthink or overanalyze situations, which is how most traders lose money. Over-analysis and overthinking leads to more trades and eventually losses

This type of trading helps to improve your time management and money management because of the set-and-forget approach that comes with it.

If you utilize, this strategy, you will avoid most of the mistakes that traders are prone to make just by virtue of being human beings. As humans, we want to trade always because it makes us feel in control and excites us, but this can prove to be fatal as the results may not always be what we want. The strategy essentially allows you to circumnavigate your faulty natural trading wiring to become a winning trader.

Most importantly, this trading method will allow you to enjoy the results of your hard work and improve your trading. Some successful traders employ this routine and find it easy to implement because it allows you to fully make use of your day, and as such, you have enough time away from the charts. Most traders prefer this routine because it means that they get away from the 9 to 5 job mentality that they found boring in the first place.

Risk management

When people go on a journey they tend to take a survival kit, the essential things that they might need. It is strange when new aspiring traders expect to succeed somehow without having the essentials of what it takes to be a successful trader. If you have all the rest, but do not have this one, you are going to fail as a trader. This one special thing that will help you to survive and eventually to prosper is risk management.

Move your stop loss orders when your trade is in profit

Another way to protect your capital and money that you have made is to move your stop loss order when your open trade is in profit. You can never be sure whether your trade will hit your expected profit target. Therefore, when you have a certain amount of pips, it is wise to move your stop loss to the profit zone. Let's say you have 100 pips of profit. You expect price will continue moving further, but you can never be sure. You may move your stop loss order and lock in some profit in case price moves against you. In the example of 100 pip profit you may lock in 50 pips, just to be sure you do not lose everything you have made.

So, I hope you see importance of protecting your capital. Learn this lesson now and it will help you save your capital and possibly your trading career later.

Using a stop loss is not a choice

One of the things that can help you to control your risk is to use a stop loss order. Trading without a stop loss is a sure way to disaster. There are a lot of various fundamental events that happen from time to time and markets start crashing in a matter of seconds. A stop loss maybe the only thing which will help you to survive that!

What is recommended stop loss percentage?

It is clear that if you want to make money you have to risk it. The problem is: how much. Most investors agree that 2 percent of equity is just about the right amount of money that you can risk on a single trade. If you are planning to open a few positions, you still have to be sure that the total risk percentage on all your open trades would not be higher than 2 percent.

Never risk all of your capital on a single trade

I have heard a lot of stories how traders risked all of their capital on a single trade expecting to make a killing and they actually lost it all. If you expect to do the same, I have a good piece of advice; better go to the casino and play roulette. There is no difference between risking it all on a single trade and gambling at a casino.

You need to protect your capital, because capital is the thing that you are going to make money with. Your money is the tool that helps you to make money. If you push it "all in" and lose, you lose the tool that helps you to make money. You can't afford to be doing that. You need to remember one thing, before you learn how to make money in currencies you have to learn how to protect it.

You also have to remember that you are going to experience good and bad days. You will sometimes experience a "losing streak" when you have a number of trades (in a row) that you are going to close with a loss. If you do not risk much you are going to survive those streaks, if you risk too much you will fail sooner rather than later.

You have not only to make money, but to protect it.

In most businesses making money and saving money are two things that help you to go on. If you make a lot, but spend even more, you are not really successful and you won't survive as a businessman. Your business will fail. You need to save some of what you make in case something goes wrong.

The same is true with investing with currencies. You not only have to make money to be successful, but you need to protect your capital and what you make if you want to be in the market for the long haul. To start with you should know statistics. Around 80 percent of traders lose all of their invested money in currencies within a year. Most of them, actually, lose it within the first few months of their trading. Why? There are a lot of reasons, but the main is that they risk too much of their capital on trades.

Have a stop loss

No matter what type of trading you are doing, whether it is Forex trading, investing or any other type of trade, you should make sure that you have a stop loss in place so that you can make the best decision possible. The stop loss will prevent you from having a

58

problem with your trades and will also give you the chance to see that there is so much more to trading than losing money. The stop loss will keep you from losing money up to a certain amount and will give you the options that you need to make sure that you are getting the best experience possible.

If you want to make sure that you are protected, a stop loss is the only way that you are able to do so. It can help save you from having major problems that are often associated with unregulated trading and with the way that many people lose money just from starting out in their trade career.

Keep learning markets

Learning to Trade on Forex

So far, you know the basics of forex trading. However, how can one learn how to trade well in the forex market? Luckily, there are a few tips to help you become a better forex trader.

Look for a Mentor

Finding a mentor who can guide you to learn how to trade in forex and make a profit is not that easy. In fact, it is rare to find ads or information about forex mentoring. So you have the biggest task. If you have a trader that you follow, then you can decide to ask him whether they can be your mentor. Some may refuse because they don't have that time. Others may decline because they don't have the skills to mentor. Regardless of all these challenges, a mentor is the right person to help you learn how to trade in Forex. A mentor will guide you while you trade so that you don't make glaring mistakes that should affect you.

That said; look for a mentor who has gained a few skills and knowledge in the forex market. It is not the role of a mentor to teach you the basics of forex trading. Instead, a mentor should help you learn how to trade successfully.

Another thing to consider before picking a mentor is to identify your favorite trading style that you want to learn. That means if you prefer technical analysis; look for a mentor who trades using this technique. Your goal should be to learn how to trade long-term and not short-term. That is why you should not waste time looking for help from day traders, always go for long-term investors.

Learn To Trade on a Demo Account

Much has been discussed about using a demo trading account. To reinforce whatever was said before, the best way to test a new trading strategy is on a demo account. If it is your first time to forex trade, use a demo account to learn how leverage works. Find out how a spread changes for different forex pairs.

Read Trading Resources

Forex trading knowledge is crucial for one to thrive in forex trade. Reading trading books helps you develop better ideas on how to trade forex. When you learn a trading idea, you must practice it in the live market.

Watch Webinars

There are a few great free webinars. Besides this, you'll find webinars organized by certain forex brokers. A few of these webinars feature technical analysis while others are about fundamental analysis.

Enroll for a Course

The one fact about forex trading is that most traders are losing money daily. Brokers know this, and that is why some have a free trading course. Successful traders teach most of these courses. Of course, not all classes are free. There are some that you have to pay a certain fee before you get permission to access it. The choice is all yours whether you want to pay for it or not.

Follow Other Traders on Social Networks

The modern era features social networks. These are great places to chat with your fellow traders. Some of these networks feature valuable information that is good for a new trader. If you are on Twitter, look for traders using the hashtags and other keywords. In most of these social networks, you'll find traders who are ready to share out their thoughts about the current market. Sometimes, they may tweet or post interesting chart or link.

Forums

Most forums have people who talk bullshit. Well, if you like discussions, then join them. Maybe you could be lucky to find good traders who can guide you to become a better trader.

What is the bottom line?

The best lesson is that there is no single trading technique. It is your role to build your trading system. With time, you have to change the way of trading. To be successful, you must be ready to learn from other successful traders. Copy what they do. That way, there is hope for you to make it in forex trading.

Chapter 8: Dividend Stocks

Overview of the stock market

Now, the question of "What is investing?" can be quite difficult to answer. In a nutshell, it's quite similar to going to buy your first car on a budget.

When you're buying a car, you already know how much you are willing to pay at the most and your ceiling is set. You also want to get the best car you can for the money, rather than being stuck with something like a lemon.
When you're looking for investments, you want to get the most bang for your buck. This should also be done without exposing yourself to more risk than necessary. In this case, a lemon would be a stock that doesn't pay out. After all, it serves your purposes about as well as a lemon does for driving around town.
Now, when you invest, you'll have a wide variety of choices when it comes to where you want to put your money. Stocks, bonds, mutual funds, or even currencies are all forms of investment. On the other hand, dividend investments are a healthy balance between these for many investors.
Occasionally, there can be quite a bit of risk. However, in those situations the returns tend to be massive if the risk ever does pay off. Investors get benefits when the share price increases, as well as being able to get profits through dividends rather than having to sell their shares like most other kinds of investors.
In this chapter, we'll discuss what dividend investing is at the base level. We will start from the very bare bones beginning of answering the question "What is a dividend?"

Dividend Stocks

Dividend stocks are, well, stocks that pay out dividends. Dividends in turn, are payments, which are made in either currency or shares, which are given to shareholders for supporting the company.
By using dividend payments, a given company will distribute a certain portion of their profits to the shareholders every quarter of the year. Later, the company puts some of the money gained from this back into the company, which will fuel their growth.
The percentage of profits that a company pays out in dividends is dubbed the payout ratio.
In order to be a successful dividend investor, you need to understand what drives companies to pay out dividends. For a company to be a success, it needs to make more money than it loses. When a company makes money, it has multiple avenues where it can spend it:

-Reinvesting it: Companies can put their money back into their businesses, which is called reinvesting. This is usually done with the agenda of growing the business to increase profits.

-Pay debt: In addition to selling their shares, companies sometimes borrow money from banks or other companies in order to raise capital. Companies will also sometimes use these profits to buy shares back from some of their investors. This is usually done when they feel like it is undervalued. Some more skilled CEO's will also trigger buyouts to artificially inflate share prices.

-Pay Dividends: Paying dividends is a way for a company to share profits and this spreads wealth throughout the company's owners, who are the shareholders. The policies regarding dividends generally reflects how the board of directors wants to use their profits.

Popularity of dividends

For hundreds of years, long-term investors invested in dividend stocks. At the beginning of the 20th century, most of the money made in the stock market in the US came in the form of dividends that companies paid to their shareholders. It is one of the opportunities that an average investor can enjoy now too. This age is dominated by speculation in various securities. People tend to believe that they can make a killing in the stock market by selecting the right stock that would rise by a thousand percent and they will win a jackpot. Unfortunately, most speculators end up losing it all. They ignore long-term profits and tend to choose short-term strategies to invest in stocks. Very few investors now think about a company in terms of whether it pays dividends or not. Most are searching for growth stocks that start their existence in the market from $5 or something and in a matter of a few years, skyrocket to $100 or even more. They search for future CISCO, Wal-Mart, Apple or Google that are going to fly like rockets to the moon and will make them wealthy beyond their wildest dreams. Very few find these stocks. Some pick up some penny stocks and lose a substantial amount of their money investing in them.

However, the facts speak for themselves. Some say that for the past 100 years or so, more than forty percent of the famous S&P500 returns came from dividends. The statistics should make one think whether or not it is better to leave short-term strategies and concentrate on the long-term ones. One of the best strategies is, of course, investing in dividend stocks. When you start delving into the subject, you will see how many advantages this kind of investing has over other most popular trading strategies. Let us look through some of the benefits of buying and holding dividend-paying stocks.

You earn from dividends and from rising share prices.

So, this shows that there is a possibility to make money in two ways. Firstly, you get dividends and most are paid quarterly. Secondly, you can also make substantial amount of money from a rise in your shares. As you know, stocks rise and fall and since you are in these special dividend stocks for the long haul, you are surely going to benefit in these two ways: from steady dividends and from rising prices of your shares.

Steady income year after year

Those who only expect to make money as shares rise will often have to sit out through bear markets when all stocks are falling and they do not get the privilege of getting steady income from the market in those times. However, those who own dividend stocks can enjoy never-ending streams of cash in good times and bad. Even if the price of your shares is falling, your dividends are still paid and your steady stream of income never stops.

The power of compounding when reinvesting your dividends

Some investors talk about the power of compounding that they get when they reinvest the dividends.. In a nutshell, compounding is getting current/future earning from previous earnings. So, if you get dividends and you use them to buy more shares of a company that pays them, next time you will get more dividends (and consequently more cash). If you invest those, you will again get more shares and more dividends. These earning will keep growing tremendously if you continue doing this year after year until you retire and have probably created yourself a nest egg.

This type of investment protects your wealth from losing its value during inflation

We do know that during inflation, money starts losing its value. As prices grow, your money gets less and less power to buy things due to rising prices. For centuries, investors have tried to protect their hard-earned cash from depreciation by investing in gold and in dividend stocks. Inflation often follows an overheated economy when everything is booming and various new businesses spring up. That's when companies make bigger profits and consequently pay more significant dividends. Your price of shares rises and so do the dividends.

Dividend stocks outperform those that do not pay dividends

Growth stocks may do very well during booms. However, as fast as they rise, they plummet when financial bubbles burst. Those who have held to those stocks often lose all of their profits and even more. Dividend stocks may not take you for such an extraordinary ride upwards, but they will also not take you down hard when the economy heads south. So, those who follow long-term investment strategies and do not jump in and out of the market, trying to get a quick buck will earn cash in good times and bad. Value stocks that they hold make them money even during very bad times, because dividends do not stop coming. On the other hand, those who have been following short-term strategies have no streams of income from the market in bad times and they need to wait for another boom in order to make money from rising prices in stocks.

These stocks provide you with financial safety and stability

As people grow older, they want less risk and more stability and security. That is precisely what investing in dividend stocks is all about. You protect yourself from falling markets by still keeping a steady stream of income. Prices of these stocks are often cheaper, but as dividends rise together with prices of shares, you earn more and more. In the same fashion as gold, dividend stocks have proven to be one of the safest ways to invest in the stock market.

It relieves you from the pressure of where to enter and exit the market

Short-term investors are very concerned as to where they have to enter and exit the market. They intend to capitalize on fast stock price moves and it is crucial to be right on time when the move starts. Long-term dividend investors do not have to worry about that. They simply select the best paying dividend stocks and accumulate their wealth slowly but surely. They do not have psychological pressure regarding daily market fluctuations as they know they are there for the long haul.

Diversification

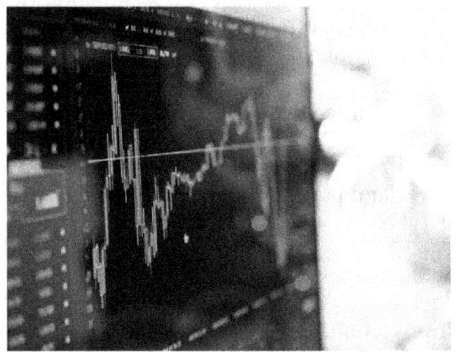

Many dividend investors diversify their portfolios through dividend exchange traded funds (ETFs). Basically, ETFs allow you to invest in a basket of high-dividend paying stocks.

Dividend ETFs are mainly established to achieve high yields when investing in high-dividend-paying real-estate investment trusts (REITs), preferred stocks, or common stocks.

Most dividend ETFs may contain only US stocks or they could be composed of international ETFs with a global focus. Many indexes used to build the dividend ETFs contain stocks with higher than average liquidity and above-market dividend yields. But take note that these will vary based on the fund manager of the ETF and their particular style.

Dividend ETFs are managed passively, which means they are monitoring a particular index, that is often filtered based on quantitative criteria to involve companies with a solid track record of dividend increases and more established blue-chip companies that are basically regarded to carry minimal risk.

The expense to dividend ratio must be lower or at least at par to the most affordable no-load mutual funds. By definition, you can buy or redeem no-load mutual funds after a specific duration of time without sales or commission charge. In general, dividend ETFs are ideal for risk-averse stock investors who are mainly seeking income.

Dividend ETFs Vs Other ETFs

In general, ETFs will provide you the opportunity to diversify an index fund and enable minimal trades as they don't have minimum deposit requirements. Moreover, the expense ratios of ETFs are lower compared to average mutual funds for commonly available ETFs in the stock market.

Adding dividend ETFs to your overall investment portfolio will provide you robust yet safe financial strategy, but there are also other forms of ETFs that you may consider and include in your portfolio for further diversification.

For instance, an Initial Public Offering (IPO) ETF can be enticing for investors who like to try investing in startup companies who are opening their business to the public. You can diversify your investment across different IPOs from different industries and sectors.

The benefits of investing in IPO ETFs are grounded in the upsides from possible beneficial growth in the stock price. However, initial IPO success doesn't guarantee stability and growth because the value of the holdings may decrease eventually. And of course, very few startup companies will offer dividend payouts on the onset so you have to think carefully of including this in your portfolio.

Meanwhile, Index ETFs monitor a benchmark index such as the S&P 500. You can trade index ETFs all day long on a primary stock exchange and you can take advantage of exposure to different securities in a single transaction.

Depending on the ETF you are tracking, index ETFs may include both American and international markets, different asset classes or specific sectors.

Lastly, the ETF of ETFs is mainly tracking other ETFs instead of an index or an underlying stock. This special type of ETF will provide you more opportunities for diversification compared to other ETFs.

ETF of ETFs are managed actively similar to funds in comparison with other ETFs that are managed passively. Thus, they can be designed to consider other factors such as your time horizon and risk tolerance. This approach will provide you with wide exposure to strategies across various class assets, immediate diversification, and minimal charges.

Building a dividend portfolio is part science, part art. This significantly depends on your available capital, risk tolerance, and goals. Taking a closer look at the important risk factors could affect the returns of a portfolio and could help you avoid taking unnecessary risk.

Below are risk management pointers that you should bear in mind:

Stocks must be diversified across various sectors and industries, with no specific sector composing more than 25% of the value of the portfolio.

Stocks with high financial leverage and higher volatility usually pose a greater risk for stockholders.

Depending on due diligence constraints and portfolio size, holding between 20 and 60 well-balanced stocks is reasonable for individual investors.

Small cap stocks have high volatility compared to large cap stocks

A stock beta will help you determine the volatility of the stock in relation to the market

You are basically speculating if you invest with a time horizon in months or quarters

Low risk

The stocks you have identified through relative dividend strategy tend to have lower risk than the rest of the companies in the market because these are often stocks that are ignored.

When relative dividend strategy identifies a possible investment, the stock is already underperforming in the market for quite some time. There is a low possibility that the share price will fall further because it has already experienced a dramatic drop.

Dividends and retirement

Living off dividends depends significantly on when you want to retire as well as the lifestyle which you look forward to maintaining. For instance, an individual may have a goal to retire in his 50s and spend his time traveling around the world. This may differ for another investor that is looking forward to retiring at the standard age and wants a steady flow of income post-retirement to cover expenses. Both of these retirement plans cater to different amounts of expected income, hence a different percentage of savings and investments.

For someone wanting to retire early, they'd need to invest a higher percentage of their income on a monthly basis compared to someone looking for just a little cushion apart from their pension.

The current generation is expected to be aggressively invested in passive sources of income and have a consistent retirement plan in place. However, it is suggested that not more than 50 percent of the savings must be invested in stocks.

Four Percent Rule of Retirement

This rule sets a limit on how much a retiree should ideally withdraw from their retirement account every passing year. This rule helps maintain balance with investment and income stream for retirees. 4% withdrawal rate is considered by experts to be safe and sufficient to long term investment, and savings plans as the withdrawal will likely only consist of interest and dividends rather than the initial investment amount that can continue to grow.

How To Retire Through Dividend (Living Off Dividends)

The biggest reason anyone wants to get into the world of investing – especially in the dividend sector of the market – is usually so that they can make enough money to cover the expenses that come with retirement. So there's a lot that has to be done to prepare for that day you decide you don't want to do a full 40-hour work week anymore, which starts with deciding which strategy to go with and then fine-tuning it as the market changes over time (because what works now may not work the same way in 20 years).

How to reach those goals is focused on the type of dividend investing that generates good cash flow for multiple decades, and that's easily done by following these guidelines.

Always Contribute to Your Portfolio

The first rule is to continuously add money into your dividend profile, preferably some out of every paycheck or a higher amount every month. What happens is that investors are allowed to average the expense of their value over the course of several years.

This provides the ability to build a dividend folder, which doesn't require the need to purchase all of your current stock in one single lump sum; it often isn't always the best option for those looking forward to retirement.

If people ignore it, then the benefits are limited as they are only building what is already there. Even though you will find there's reinvestment option, you'll stand to make all the more money faster with the help of adding more into your investments. Think about that when you get that third cup of coffee shop brew that you average per morning.

Seek Out a Dependable Dividend

The second rule is to maintain a focus on dividend growth stocks, which come from companies that usually offer a consistent raise of rates in distribution to the shareholders. If you want to have your dividend payouts cover your expenses while you are relaxing on the beaches of Maui, then you will want to have a dependable company to invest in for those long periods.

That's why investors attempt to find ways to avoid the risk of inflation and put their money in stocks that they can afford to increase their payouts on if they ever need to.

Buy Quality - Not Necessarily Quantity

This task is bringing the savings into a brokerage account pertaining to additional investments. It means that a good investor should build a collection of standard screening criteria so that you can have a report on dividend leaders, as well as achieves – this is long unless you can trim the list to a more manageable amount.

One of what considered is in case a company offers a lot more than 2. 5 percent, dividends that have observed rises for at the very least 10 years in a row and trading under 20 times already in the market. While some may pun intended, the larger payout ratios – indicative that the company is benefiting a produce spike that won't last for a longer time (you wouldn't much like the dip on this roller coaster) – which could change with respect to the industry the company you happen to be potentially investing falls under.

Quality can become determined after careful research from the details for each stock. This helps the investor figure out whether the stock options offer enough to provide a rising revenue rate and correlating dividend obligations over for at least some decades to come. A properly diversified portfolio will provide good success for the different income stocks which you carefully picked.

Create a Diversified Portfolio

This is done so that you can not only lessen the risk of loss, but also shield the investor by purchasing as many stocks from numerous different companies as you can for a far more steady income that will come in handy during retirement. You don't want to keep all your eggs in one basket, as the old saying is goes. Some experts suggest an investor's stock portfolio should include almost 30 individual companies across many industries.

Think of a retail center and the amount of stores one usually has. They don't just have restaurants or department stores. There are specialty stores for gaming fans, photography folks, craftsmen, sports supporters, baby clothes, toys and almost everything in between. Would a mall using 20 or 35 Starbucks sound extremely fun? It likely wouldn't be extremely successful.

Reinvest Wisely

When it comes to putting your money back into your dividend portfolio, don't do it too soon, and let your dividends build up. This is where the power of compounding interest comes into play, where you are gaining more money in a shorter time. Not everyone uses that strategy, and most will likely hold their money for safer reinvestments and keep them with the steady growths.

Chapter 9: Concepts of Dividend Investing

Main Advantages of Dividend Investing
Getting dividends is like a miniature version of being a bank. It's much like collecting money from your savings account. While it is a very nice thing, it isn't that exciting. Betting on how shares will rise and fall is a much more exciting thing to do, especially when share prices skyrocket. If we put excitement aside, it's much more lucrative. If you're looking for a fix, together with dividend investing, then you might want to pursue riskier companies that, at the moment, have higher growth rates.
Dividend investing also has a few obvious advantages over other types of investing:
It's passive income - Dividends will give you a steady flow of passive income. You can then pick and choose what to do with this money. If you've got a lot of money to start with, you might just live comfortably. Otherwise, you might choose to reinvest this, maybe even into some riskier stocks to dabble in day or swing trading. On the other hand, the passive income makes dividend investing the best sort of investing for retirees.
Companies are more stable - Dividend investing companies are those that are generally much more mature and stable. After all, it can take quite a bit of money to be able to afford this. You'll rarely (let's not say never) find a startup that pays out dividends. Dividends are generally paid only when the company is established. On the other hand, startups put pretty much all of their money into growth. Dividend payments are only profitable for bigger companies because it helps the board of directors have a steady flow of income. Furthermore, paying dividends makes managers more accountable, and shareholders less likely to sell out.
The risk is lower - Dividend investing gives you two ways to make a return on your money. Either just reaping the dividend payments, or simply selling your stocks. This is why it generally has a much lower risk than say, day trading. The market is also less volatile, which can cause stocks to rise during times of recession.
It's more liquid - Let's compare dividend investments to just buying stocks. You can

achieve a positive ROI either by simply sitting and taking the benefits of your dividends or selling out stocks at a higher point than you entered. In a day trading setting, your only way of achieving returns is selling high and buying low. This can sometimes make it quite difficult to liquidate your assets.

You have a vote in the company - One of the most frustrating parts of getting a company's shares is that you have no control over the company's decisions. As a shareholder, you do. You're able to have at least a small vote in what the company does in the future, which can help you attain bigger profits on your own merit.

Cash buys more shares - When you buy a given number of shares in a company that doesn't pay out dividends, all you get is a number of shares. If you want more than you already have, you have to take more money in order to buy them. On the other hand, dividend investing will let you buy more shares by reinvesting the dividends you get. You don't have to go into your pocket a second or third time to get more shares in the company. Many companies even offer special benefits for reinvesting your dividends into the company.

It helps against inflation - Even a moderate rate of inflation can usually take a large amount of your earnings. For example, if you earn 10%, but the inflation rate is 3% you've only really earned 7% of profits. On the other hand, when inflation makes companies charge more for their products, dividends rise proportionally, meaning that a 7% return is usually a lot closer to 10%.

It's great for bear markets - In a market that's exhibiting bearish movements, when share prices are flat or dropping, companies that pay dividends still have to pay out dividends. These dividends generally help you make up for any loss accrued, and sometimes even turn out positive.

Baby Boomer Boost - The Baby Boomer Boost is a term that has been coined by economists to refer to the predicted rise in value of dividend stocks when baby boomers reach retirement age. Now, nobody can predict which year, or even which decade this is going to happen in, but it is something that's good to be aware of in the next few decades.

Risk Will Always Exist

While dividend investing is one of the lowest risk kinds of investment, it still exposes you to some risk. "Safe" investments don't really exist. There are only safer and riskier investments, and there are still plenty of ways to lose money when dividend investing, such as:

Share prices dropping - This can happen regardless of whether or not the company you're investing in pays dividends. Naturally, those are more stable, but no company is ever truly stable. In the worst case scenario, the company might go belly-up before you've even had an inkling of a chance to sell out.

Dividend cuts - Companies are able to cut down dividend payment rates whenever they want to. Companies are, legally at least, not obliged to pay dividends or increase the payments they make to investors. Unlike bonds, where when there's a failure to pay interest, you can put a company at fault, dividend payments can be cut or deleted whenever a company wants to do this. If you're counting on a single stock to pay dividends, you might view this as losing your money. Naturally, companies are prone to avoiding this because it tends to make shareholders sell out.

Inflation is still present - While your income isn't getting affected by inflation that much, the same doesn't go for your savings. If you don't reinvest your money, or invest in something that doesn't keep pace with inflation, then your investment capital is actually losing value. With inflation, every single penny you save will be worth a bit less in a year's time. The potential risk of your investment is, generally at least, proportional to its returns. If you put all your money in a FDIC insured bank, which pays interest more than inflation, your money will retain value. On the other hand, that won't make you rich.

If you take a gamble on a high-growth company, you can sometimes get a massive return on investment. This is naturally also quite risky. After all, if getting rich was a risk-free endeavor, everyone would do it instantly.

In the following section, this is exactly what we'll be dealing with. Every investor has an amount of risk they're willing to take, as well as an amount of risk that they aren't quite as eager to take on. It's important to find where yours lies, because that's pretty much the lifeblood of your career as a dividend investor.

Compound interest

The most important concept of investing is the time value of money, and it's very easy to understand. A dollar invested today is worth more than that same dollar invested ten years from today, because if you wait to invest, then you miss out on all those years of returns. This is the reason why we're all encouraged to start saving for retirement at such a young age. And it's also the reason why we have to pay interest whenever we borrow money. If you took Finance 101 in college, they probably had you set up an amortization table to forecast the return on investment, or they gave you a formula that accomplishes the same end without the burden of formatting a spreadsheet.

It's important to understand that there's a difference between the interest that compounds for us and interest that compounds against us. When we invest in stocks, receive dividends, and then reinvest the dividends, the interest is compounding for us, and over time our returns are multiplied. Say we have $5,000 invested in a stock that yields 3%. Over a year, we'll receive a dividend income of $150. If we reinvest the $150, it brings our total holdings up to $5,150. Now the 3% yield is applied to $5,150 in holdings rather than just the initial $5,000. Throughout the second year, we'll receive a dividend income of $154.50. So by reinvesting our dividends, we received an extra $4.50. This might seem small, but that's okay. We've just started to compound, and this is a long-term strategy. In real life, that stock price will change (hopefully for the better) as well as the dividend payment (again, we hope for the better). But let's ignore this impact and focus just on compounding. If the price and dividend yield remains constant, at the end of 10 years, our investment will be worth $6,719.58 and will provide an annual dividend income of $201.59. After 20 years, our investment will be worth $9,030.56 and will provide an annual dividend income of $270.92. After 30 years, the investment will reach $12,136.31 and pay an annual dividend of $364.09.

In real life, there are other variables to consider. The company might cut its dividend. It might stay the same, or it might raise the dividend every single year. The price of the stock will fluctuate and also succumb to long-term trends. Maybe it will trend down. Maybe it will trend up. To make an investment in the stock, we should have some confidence that both the price and dividend payment will increase. This won't always happen, but if we invest in a portfolio of carefully selected dividend payers, we can expect to receive, on average, capital gains and larger dividends that make the results even better than what is illustrated above. The same concept applies to bonds and real estate, given that interest and rents compound the same way if reinvested.

It's nice to be on the receiving end of an interest payment. But that's not always the case. When we borrow money to acquire possession, the interest works against us, and over time the amount we have to pay is also multiplied. Credit card debt is the most prevalent example of interest compounding against the borrower. At the time of writing this, the average credit-card-carrying American is holding the debt of $5,839, meaning, of course, that some people carry no debt while others carry significantly more. And those carrying debt are holding it month after month, perhaps chipping away at it over time, or maybe allowing it to grow even more out of control. But anyone who carries a balance isn't just paying interest on the price of their purchases; they're also paying interest on the balance that exists at the end of each month. In other words, they pay interest on whatever interest they haven't paid yet. And this allows the debt to keep getting bigger and bigger.

Debt isn't necessarily bad, but with credit card debt, it almost always is. There's a huge difference between taking on debt to acquire a consumable item, like just about every credit card purchase and taking on debt to acquire an asset that will appreciate in value, such as a home. Yes, the interest on your mortgage will compound against you, but you're also buying your home with hopes that it will appreciate in value.

When you first take out a mortgage, the overwhelming majority of each payment goes towards interest, and just a small portion goes towards reducing the principal. Over time, the principal will get smaller and smaller, and the result is that each payment is then composed of less interest and more principal. The faster you pay off the principal, the less interest you pay over the life of the loan. In this circumstance, I'm going to say that the homebuyer benefits from taking out a loan for two important reasons. One, it's possible that the home will increase in value by more than the amount of interest paid, so in this regard, the buyer has incurred the interest expense to acquire assets that will return more than the cost of the house and interest combined. And two, one of the benefits of buying a home is the free rent that goes along with it. You don't have to write a check to your landlord each month, and assuming the home appreciates in value, you get your money back when you sell it. The mortgage payment is very different than rent in that it is likely to provide a return later in life.

The successful dividend investor does so much more than just buy dividend stocks; they make sure that they're playing for the right team. It's all about earning interest rather than paying interest, and if you structure your finances appropriately, then a mixture of interest, dividends, and rents should work for you instead of against you. Compound interest is indeed a powerful tool when it comes to wealth accumulation. Albert Einstein once said, "Compound interest is the eighth wonder of the world. He who understands it earns it, he who doesn't pay it". Success in any endeavor isn't a single action. It's a series of smart decisions that you have to keep making over and over again to build your success. If you want to be successful in building wealth by investing in dividend-paying assets, you have to reinvest the dividends.

76

Revenue

At the top of the Income Statement is revenue. Comparing revenue from the current year to prior years will provide an indication as to whether or not the company is growing. Ideally, we want to see revenues increase from one year to the next. Obviously, the bigger the year-over-year increase, the better. And any increase that scarcely keeps pace with inflation should not be considered an increase at all. Revenue is metrics for demand. It speaks directly to the number of sales generated by the company. It does not tell us anything about how efficiently the company generated those sales. If revenue is decreasing and the company makes corresponding cuts to their expenses, the bottom line (net income) may very well increase. And while such a situation would increase profits (for the year), it's an indication that growth has stagnated. For a stock to be an attractive investment, we don't just want to see an increase to net income, but also want to see revenue increasing each year.

Gross profit

Gross profit is a company's revenue minus the cost incurred to generate that revenue. It's beneficial to see this number increase along with the revenue, meaning that the company is not increasing costs by too much to generate additional sales. If sales are increasing, gross profit will tell us if the company was able to increase those sales by more or less than the corresponding increase in the cost of sales.
To compare gross profit between different companies, calculated as a ratio: Gross Profit / Revenue = Gross Profit Margin
This type of comparison is most meaningful when made between companies in the same industry. The higher the margin in comparison to that of the company's competitors, the better.

Income statement

The income statement can be used to analyze a company's revenues (or sales) and the expenses that are not only attributed directly to those sales but the overall operations of the company. In general terms, it allows us to analyze how effectively the company generates sales, and how efficiently it manages expenses.

Balance sheet

While the income statement is our source of information for earnings, the balance sheet tells us about the company's overall financial position. How many assets has the company accumulated? What kind of debt is it currently holding? And do assets exceed liabilities in providing a positive equity position? These are the types of questions we'll be asking.
The entire balance sheet should be reviewed before making an investment. But different companies will show different types of assets and liabilities, especially if they compete in different industries. If one company manufactures a good while another provides a service, there will be items on their balance sheets that are not comparable. For this reason, we are going to home in on an assortment of key items that every investor should be familiar with. We'll look at both assets and liabilities, knowing that in an accounting sense, the true worth of the company is net assets or assets held in excess of liabilities. Assets – Liabilities = Owner's Equity
The owner's equity represents the value of the company, but this measurement is

different from how the company is valued on a stock exchange. In exchange, the company is worth whatever the investors are willing to pay for it (or, more specifically, what the most recent investor paid for it). The current selling price multiplied by the number of shares outstanding determines the market capitalization. But accountants aren't concerned with what investors are willing to pay for the company; they want to know the valuation of what the company owns less the obligations they've incurred but have yet to pay.

If we take the owner's equity and divide by the number of shares outstanding, we get the book value per share. This, of course, will differ from what a share of stock sells for an exchange. In most cases, the market price per share will exceed the book value per share. And this is perfectly fine. Most value investors don't mind paying more than book value. Ben Graham, the father of value investing, advocated buying stocks with a price-to-book ratio of 1.5 or less, meaning he was only willing to pay 1.5 times the book price for a share of stock. Given this criterion, if we find a stock with a price-to-book ratio of less than 1.5 or even less than 1, it should be a candidate for investment. Other attributes, such as a solid profit margin or a strong outlook for growth, are likely more important than book value. So when you find a stock with an attractive price-to-book ratio, consider it is the icing on the cake.

Operating expenses

Operating expenses include necessary expenses to support the company's operations. Unlike the cost of revenue, these expenses won't fluctuate directly with output. Operating expenses include rent, research and development, the cost of equipment, administrative payroll, insurance, and a large host of expenses that a company incurs regardless of that quarter's production run. Generally, a company will attempt to reduce these costs as a means of staying efficient and competitive, or if the company is struggling, they'll reduce them just to stay alive. An increase in operating expenses can be an indication of coming improvements in the quality or innovation of their products or services. Or it can mean that they are slipping in terms of efficiency.

Dividend growth

When investing in dividends, you can become a simple dividend investor or a dividend growth investor. The latter often entails investing in unsustainable stocks offering very high dividend yields. Such striking stocks are often struggling to maintain their footing and want to attract investors by all means, something you already know.

You also know that as a smart investor, you have to be willing to start low with the most enjoyable element to dividends —which is their ability to grow— at the back of your mind.

Looking for companies that increase their dividends over time has also shown to have benefits in terms of security (of the company) and stock price in bad economic times.

Before we delve deeper, let us make sure you understand the difference between a dividend growth investor and a simple dividend investor.

The advantages of dividend growth investing

Here are the benefits of dividend growth investing.

Your income grows ahead of inflation

Imagine a situation where you are looking forward to retiring on dividends, and suddenly, your income fails to increase when inflation cripples the markets.

As the years go by, you would be worse off —and probably even have to start over with another hasty, consolatory passive income stream to make up for the lost effort, money, and time. That is the reason why bond prices react so poorly when the tiniest hint of future inflation comes about.

Generally, bonds are a 'fixed income' because they have a fixed coupon, which means the payouts do not increase. Dividends that increase with inflation means that your income will always have protection in real terms.

A good dividend grower will help you with compound interest

With dividend growers, compound interest will work for you in many ways. For instance, the company itself harnesses the power of compound interest effectively as they re-invest the retained incomes for you, which results in more revenue in the future.

Secondly, you get to re-invest the dividends you get so that you can purchase more shares in the same business or in a different company to help you grow your future income.

Something to note:

Remember that for dividend growth to be sustainable, the company has to invest the past profits —that they did not disburse to their shareholders— or the retained earnings to increase their earnings per share over time. Doing this ensures the earnings per share increase over time. They get to invest their retained earnings by investing in the business —for instance, by increasing the capital expenditure, buying new companies, or even buying back their shares— which automatically means increased earnings per share (or reducing the interest charge to reduce their debt).

You should be very keen on selecting companies with a record of earnings stability, a strong dividend history, pricing power, and a high return on equity.

Before we discuss a standout strategy in dividend investing, we have to talk a little about something we mentioned (lightly) earlier: the dividend payout ratio in dividend growth.

Recurring events and non-recurring

Non-Recurring Events

Sometimes a company looks really good in certain areas, yet for some reason, it has a negative net income for the year. Or maybe they underperformed in terms of sales, but net income still went up. In either case, you'll want to take a look at the numbers booked under non-recurring events. These are one-time happenings that impact the bottom line. That amazing real estate deal alluded to above is a non-recurring event. It's also an example of the company making money. Another year there might be a natural disaster that destroys one of their plants. This, of course, would produce a loss. If a non-recurring event leads to a loss, you want to dig deeper. It might be necessary to wade through the 10K and review the footnote disclosures. But if it's a large company with heavy coverage, then a Google search might be an easier way to see what's going on. It could be a write-off of bad debt with no expected impact on future performance. Or it could be the result of litigation against the company, and depending on the nature of the litigation, there could be a residual effect that hurts their reputation and impacts future sales. If the company has discontinued operations, it could explain why sales have fallen. But it could also be a sign that they're taking steps to improve efficiency. The numbers are just that — numbers. The interpretation is up to the investor. Reading financial statements in conjunction with articles published on the company often provides the needed insight. In this regard, larger companies with plenty of press coverage are much easier to evaluate. A non-recurring event won't always influence your perception of the company, but if they have non-recurring events each year, and the losses are significant, it's a sign to stay away.

Net income

Net income, often referred to as the bottom line, is sales (of all kinds, not just for the product or service that the company specializes in) less every expense incurred, from those required to produce or provide their product or service down to the cost of financing their operations and the interest and taxes they incurred in this endeavor. While it's important to review the bottom line, an understanding of how the above pieces feed into net income is far more important. When reviewing a large number of companies, it might be tempting to start with net income and move on to your next candidate if you don't see year-to-year improvement. I recommend starting with revenue instead. Look first for companies that have increased their revenue for at least three years straight, and don't waste any time with companies that haven't. If they pass this requirement, then keep reading and see if you're still interested by the time you've worked your way down to net income. If you are, then it's time to review the balance sheet.

Just as we did with gross profit and income from continuing operations, we can express net income as a percentage of revenue to make comparisons across companies:

Net Income / Revenue = Net Income Margin

As before, we're looking for a high ratio relative to that of the company's competitors.

Chapter 10: Investing plan

Define your funding

If you are going to invest in an exchange-traded fund, you can buy as little as a single share to get started. This isn't the case with mutual funds. They are going to require a minimum investment. The required minimum investment isn't going to be very large, but will be at least $ 1,000 and can range as high as $ 5,000.

Fees

The fees for mutual funds can be relatively high, and besides the way that they are traded, this is one of the biggest arguments against them. A "load fee" is charged every time you buy or "redeem" shares of the fund. You don't sell shares of a mutual fund, you redeem them, that gives them back to the company that manages the mutual fund. Load fees can be quite large, going as high as 8%. That is huge when you consider the practically nonexistent fees of exchange-traded funds. Moreover, load fees can be complicated. There are front-end load fees charged when you buy the shares, and back-end load fees charged when you redeem shares. Back-end load fees can be variable, depending on how long you held the shares. The longer you hold the shares, the lower the fee. So, they are encouraging you to stay in the fund.

There are also "level-load" fees that are charged once per year.

Actively Managed vs. Passively Managed Funds

Funds can be actively or passively managed. A passively managed fund is typically one that tracks a stock market index like the S & P 500. Passively managed funds, as you might guess, charge lower fees than actively managed funds. The goal of a passively managed fund is to match the return of the index that the fund tracks. Actively managed funds mean exactly what the name says; they have an active manager or managers that run the investment portfolio. As you might imagine, that costs money. The fund managers will buy and sell assets in the fund in an attempt to beat the average return of the stock market. So, they are doing what you would be doing yourself if you manage your own stock portfolio. Generally speaking, beating the average return of the stock market is not an easy task. However, some research exists showing that actively managed funds often beat the market. That said, they don't beat it by huge amounts, and the massive fees that mutual funds require can wipe out any gains from having the fund actively managed. Long term studies that have been done actually show that passively managed funds return nearly three times as much as actively managed funds.

Stock research

Once you have the preferred companies on your list, make sure to check financial performance and historical growth patterns for the companies before you make a decision to buy stocks. Some screeners provide reports as well by conducting an intelligent financial analysis. This is known as the stock-rating system. It provides analysis based on:

Dividend analysis

Efficiency

Growth

Financial strength

Growth

Stock price momentum

Brokerage research

Do your research, open a brokerage account, and start investing. You can take two main routes to invest in the stock market. You can use a full-service broker who will make investment recommendations based on your needs and wants, or an online discount or broker who will execute your orders but give you little or no advice. Discount brokers are cheaper but provide fewer services.

Invest regularly. Regular investment of a fixed amount provides a benefit called average cost in dollars. This means that during periods of the high market, you buy fewer shares. When the market is down, you will buy more shares. By investing a fixed amount each month, instead of buying a specific number of shares per month, the average cost per share will be lower.

Reduce your losses. You usually buy a stock because you think its price will go up. The problem is that you probably buy from someone who is also convinced that the stock price is falling. To build wealth in the stock market, you cannot be emotionally attached to a particular stock. Always set a stop-loss price to the amount you will lose and eliminate inventory if it falls below this level. If stock prices rise, increase your stop-loss to protect your profits.

Annual reports

A company's annual report is a decent hotspot for a considerable lot of the information things you'll require, just as for critique about the company. It ordinarily incorporates a letter from the top executive to shareholders with their view of the significant occasions influencing the company, and their view of the 66

Doing Your Homework company's possibilities going ahead. You'll likewise normally find engaging information about the company and its business (or businesses), in addition to a segment that gives all the fiscal summaries, including consolidated income proclamations, balance sheets, cash flow explanations, articulations of shareholders' equity, references, and a report of the free examiners. Perusing the annual report is an extraordinary method to acquaint yourself with a company. Remember, however, that companies attempt to put their best foot forward in their reports to shareholders, so the analysis is probably going to cast the company's situation in the most ideal light. A letter or call to a company's investor relations division is generally the entirety of that is expected to have a free duplicate of the latest annual report sent your direction.

For an apparently less one-sided view of a company's condition and prospects, you can go to one of a few stock rating productions:

• The Value Line Investment Survey gives money related information and key ratios on around 1,700 stocks and rates their attractiveness on a size of 1 to 5 for both wellbeing and timeliness.

• Standard and Poor's Stock Reports offer 67

Dividend Investing discourse and buy/hold/sell suggestions dependent on its STARS rankings for roughly 5,000 traded on an open market companies listed on the New York, American, NASDAQ, and provincial stock exchanges.

• Morningstar made its name positioning common assets; however, it has ventured into stock research through its Stock Analyst Reports on around 1,700 stocks.

In the event that you utilize a business firm, it might likewise have an assortment of stock research and proposal information accessible to you.

Look at with your delegate to discover what's offered and at what cost.

How to buy stocks

By the time you have come so far, it is safe to assume that as an investor, you have conducted complete research and are ready to invest. If your broker is charging you significantly, prefer using a non-commission-based broker. You certainly do not want to shell out a sum of money when it is comparatively easier to perform the task yourself.

Many people are in search of good ways of investment that can give them a satisfactory and a regular return but don't know where and how to make a start. So for those, we will allow them to learn about the few initial steps they need to follow before investing their life savings.

1. Decide through which form you want to invest in stocks

There is more than one approach that you might come across when deciding how to invest. This depends on you and how well you are aware of the process of buying and selling stocks.

If you have enough knowledge about the whole procedure and are good with the know-how of this system of the stock exchange and how it works, then you might continue with the approach of do-It-yourself. In this, you will decide on which firm you would like to invest in and how much investment will be sufficient to start with. After this, you only need a brokerage to buy you the stocks of your opted firm.

The second is for those who have little know-how and knowledge about the system of stocks and their trade. Such people would prefer to have an advisor or an agent who can process for them. He might not only advise them about which share would be more profitable to invest in, but would also offer other services like managing their low-cost investments. For this kind of approach, you shouldn't be roaming around looking for a good advisor, because almost all brokerage firms offer this service to their clients. They pick the stocks all by themselves, considering your specific goals and invest your money there.

Before moving on, you are required to make up your mind and make your final decision about which approach would be perfect for you.

2. Open an investing account

Usually, when you plan to invest in stocks, the first thing you would need is an investment account. For those who are carrying with everything on their own, a brokerage account would be a suitable one. And for those who need help and guidance, opening an account with the help of their advisor would be a sensible option.

3. Know the difference between individual stocks and exchange-traded funds

If you have opted to do all the stuff of investment and managing stocks all by yourself, then it is going to create some real difficulties for you. But don't worry, we'll figure it out for you. The first tip for you is never to forget that you don't have to complicate things and keep your stock investing simple. When it comes to investing in the stock market, you need to choose between these two types of investments, exchange-traded funds, and individual stocks.

An exchange-traded fund is a type of mutual fund that allows you to purchase smaller chunks of various stocks in just one transaction. It tracks an index and is also traded on a stock exchange like other individual stocks. In fact, from purchasing to selling, they are very much like the regular stocks sold on the stock exchange market. Moreover, they help you to build a diversified investment portfolio, as it allows you to enjoy a small share of ownership in multiple companies at the same time.

Individual stocks are preferable shares, especially for those who are new in this market. Furthermore, if you are tracking only a single firm or are interested only in buying one company's shares, then this might prove to be the safest or less risky form of investment. With this, if you wish to build a diversified portfolio, then you should definitely have a vast sum for investment and plenty of time.

4. Set a budget for your dividend stock investment

There are two most commonly and frequently asked questions by new and inexperienced investors that we are going to answer in this step:

The first question is, what is the minimum amount of money we require to start trading? The answer to that depends on the share price or how expensive those shares are. Let's suppose that you are planning to invest in the form of exchange-traded funds; in such cases, the minimum amount you need is only a hundred dollars or sometimes even less than that.

The second question is, what is the ideal amount of money I should invest? We have also mentioned it before how much you invest is completely your personal preference. You can invest a large share of your savings altogether at the same time for a diversified portfolio, or you can invest whole finance in the form of smaller chunks from time to time as you gain more understanding about the market.

Investing a large sum is recommended when you have planned for the long-term, and you are not concerned about the short-term returns. But if you are talking about individual stocks, then we would recommend you to keep less than 10 percent of your portfolio.

5. Start investing

You can begin with your investment after you have completed the steps mentioned above. But it would be much better if you could also determine some tactics and approaches. They play an important role in guiding you towards the right share and can help you in maximizing the return. Many experts recommend that try to build a bulky portfolio with limited finance, and if you believe and are certain about the potential long-term growth of the firm, then always go for choosing individual stocks.

Now that you are fully prepared, so let's consider the two ways of investing in more detail. The two ways include exchange-traded funds and individual dividend stocks.

Chose a trading mechanism

To get started, we are going to look at the three main classes of assets in the trading market. These are stocks, bonds and cash.

Stocks, bonds and cash

Stock refers to ownership in a company. There are two main stock categories: size and location. Each class has its own level of risk. In terms of size, stocks are classified as large, mid and small.

When comparing and contrasting stocks, bonds, cash and mutual funds, stocks are the riskiest of the three. There are two ways to make a profit on the stock exchange. First: as the value of the company increases, so does the value of their stock and if the value of the company decreases, the value of their stock decreases. There are also fluctuations that can be outside of the company's direct control. A crash in the market, for example, will affect everything regardless of how stable the company is internally. In general, however, when you buy an asset, your money will increase or decrease depending on the business' successes and failures. You can also make money on this investment through dividends, which are paid out when a company does well.

Bonds are the second type of investment we are going to review. A bond is a loan. The company or the government, borrows money from investors by selling a bond. It's a contract where they agree to pay back the money in a predetermined number of years with a predetermined interest rate. The US government borrows money from the people in the form of bonds. Here is how bonds work to make you money. When interest rates decrease, the bond's value increases. On the other hand, once interest rates rise, the value of the bond decreases. One significant thing to know about bonds is that the longer the terms are, the higher the risks, unlike stocks. However, as a general rule, bonds are lower risk than stocks.

Cash is the third type of investment, which is the money you put away in a 401K. This is the lowest risk investment of the three, but it doesn't mean there are no risks. The risk with cash has to do with inflation.

Mutual funds are a combination of stocks, bonds, and cash that have been selected and put together by professional advisors for a specific amount of risk, and reward. They are at a lower risk than stocks and bonds.

Now that you're familiar with the different types of assets, you can start to evaluate which one works best for you. Ideally, you want to balance risk and reward in your portfolio. You do this through diversification, which means holding lots of different types of investments. When determining how you want to diversify, it's important to remember that taking more risk will yield a higher return. You want to "buy low and sell high" as they say. Since the market fluctuates by nature, there are highs and lows over time, you want to buy a stock when the price is low, and then sell it when it's high. The general trend is for the market to go up, but it's difficult to predict the peaks and valleys along the way.

Dividend reinvestment

Several dividend reinvestment plans enable investors to buy additional shares of that company without paying any commission on top of the share price. In some cases, companies offer their shares at discount to investors according to their dividend reinvestment plan. Shares become quite cheap for investors when they don't have to pay commission, and the shares are offered at discount.

Dividend reinvestment allows traders to expand their overall returns over the longer term. For instance, a person invests in $5,000 in the company at a share price of $50. At the same time, the company offers a dividend of 2.5 percent. The investors will receive $125 in dividends at the end of the first years. This would increase its overall investment to $5,125. Let suppose, the company has the policy to increase the dividend by 5 percent each year, and the investors have reinvested all of the dividends. Thus, after twenty years, investor's total investment would be valued at $11,226, excluding the share price change.

Chapter 11: Investment Strategies

Dollar-cost averaging

Through dollar cost averaging, you can ditch the guesswork. Even when the market is down, your reinvestment strategy will allow you to buy more shares that it would when the market is following an upward trend.

Dollar cost averaging is an efficient and effective long-term investment strategy. It makes saving easy especially if you are gunning for retirement holdings and income. All you need is a small yet consistent flow of money. This will help you stand your ground despite market changes. This is how savvy dividend investors place a cap on their upside and basically lose money in the stock market.

Using this approach, the cost will be considerably less compared to the trading price of the shares during the time you are investing. This is because you are automatically buying fewer shares when the stocks are selling at higher prices and sell more when the prices are lower. Definitely, this strategy is only ideal for those who are investing with a long-term outlook, usually not shorter than five years. This will not produce results for traders who are looking for quick cash.

With a reinvestment plan, you can put the dollar-cost averaging on autopilot. You can just invest a specific dollar amount regularly. The usual outcome is that you can obtain more shares at lower prices then fewer shares at higher prices. You can do this regularly with a no-fee DRIP and you can build wealth in the most cost-efficient approach.

Not similar to the conventional way of investing that is based on acquiring a specific number of shares, DRIP investment is based on dollar amounts. A zero-fee reinvestment program makes it easy to invest even small amounts regularly. Dollar cost averaging will also impose discipline on your investment because you decide how many dollars you want to invest on a schedule that you have determined ahead.

How Dollar Cost Averaging Can Boost Your Dividend Income

The example below will help you understand how your dividend income can be

Dollar-Cost Average

Invest	$/Share	Share	Invest	$/Share	Share
$100	$12	8.3333	$100	$35	2.8571
$100	$9	11.1111	$100	$30	3.3333
$100	$30	3.3333	$100	$12	8.3333
$100	$35	2.8571	$100	$9	11.1111
$400		25.6348	$400		25.6348
Invest	$/Share	Share	Invest	$/Share	Share
$100	$9	11.1111	$100	$30	3.3333
$100	$12	8.3333	$100	$35	2.8571
$100	$30	3.3333	$100	$9	11.1111
$100	$35	2.8571	$100	$12	8.3333
$400		25.6348	$400		25.6348

Average price (based on the four investment prices) = $21.50
Average cost (based on the amount spent and the number of shares aquired) = $15.60

significantly improved if you sign up with a reinvestment program and use dollar cost averaging. In this example, we assume that you are investing in a stock that has zero fees. Let's say you are investing $100 every quarter and acquire however many shares your investment will buy at the present share price. Take a look at what will happen over time.

The price of the stock fluctuated between $9 and $35 with an average price of $21.50. However, the average cost per share was only $15.60 (i.e. $400/25.6348). You can buy more shares if the price is low and fewer shares if the price is high. This is precisely how you can buy low and sell high - the classic mantra in stock dividend investing.

Diversification

Diversification is a risk management technique, which includes different types of investments in a portfolio. The core concept behind this strategy claims that an investment portfolio composed of diverse forms of investments shall on average, pose a lower risk and yield higher returns than any individual investment found inside the portfolio.

Diversifying your portfolio can ease out the unsystematic risk events so the instruments that are performing well can neutralize the negative performance of others. Hence, the advantages of diversification hold only if the investments in the portfolio **are not correlated with each other.**

What is Unsystematic Risk?

Unsystematic risk, also known as residual risk or specific risk, is often described as the risk that is inherent in a business or industry investment. The types of unsystematic risk involve a new competitor in the market with the potential to take considerable market share from the business.

Even though investors may be able to project some sources of this inherent risk, it is not always certain to be aware of how or when the risk could affect your investment.

For instance, an investor in aged care stocks might be aware that a huge shift in retirement policy is inevitable. However, there is no way to know in advance the details of the new policy and how aged care companies and consumers will react.

Mathematical models and market studies have shown that keeping a well-diversified portfolio of 25 to 30 stocks could yield the most cost-effective level of reducing risk. Investing in more securities could yield further diversification benefits but in a remarkably smaller rate.

You can also maximize the benefits of diversification if you invest in foreign securities because they have the tendency to be less affected with your investments in the domestic market.

For instance, a financial crisis in the US economy may not reach the Australian economy. Hence, having Australian investments can provide you with an added layer of protection against the possible losses due to the US downturn.

Many individual investors have limited capital and so you may find it not easy to build a well-balanced and diversified portfolio. This is the reason why mutual funds are growing in popularity. Acquiring shares in a mutual fund can provide you with a more affordable way to diversify your portfolio.

Why Should You Build a Diversified Dividend Portfolio?

If you invest all of your money in one business, despite the promise of low risk and high returns, you will likely yield returns that are considerably different compared to the performance of the market in general.

Many investors don't have the stomach for such volatility, especially because there are several unforeseen events that may happen to put your investment at risk of being lost permanently.

Do you still remember Lehman Brothers? What about Enron? Placing all your eggs in one basket can have disastrous effects.

On the other hand, let's say you have the means to buy shares of each stock in the market. For each company or industry in your portfolio that is struggling, there is a possibility that there are more industries in your portfolio that are growing.

Hence, you don't need to depend on any single company to boost your investment returns and dividend income. Your portfolio can sustain a few unfortunate events because you have a diverse form of investments across several businesses.

As long as the United States continues to exist and thrive, there will be virtually no reason for your portfolio to completely lose its value. The stock market has been appreciating over the years and there are no indications that this will be disrupted anytime soon.

A diversified and well-balanced portfolio can help you diversify your risk exposure and achieve your investment goals. Building a portfolio begins with an understanding of the primary risk factors that affect the volatility and profitability of your dividend investments.

Important Risk Factors to Consider in Building Your Portfolio

Below are the most important factors that can influence the returns of your portfolio relative to the returns in the market:

The number of holdings

The amount of financial leverage each holding has

The correlation between holdings

The size of the market capitalization of each holding

These risk factor can remarkably affect the performance of a portfolio, especially during bearish markets. Many investors are usually not aware that they are betting against their portfolios until it benefits them.

As an example, let's say that around 50% of your portfolio is invested in small-cap energy stocks with high financial leverage. As oil production and prices followed an upward trend, your portfolio has received excellent returns with lower volatility as of late 2014.

Many investors would often cite their skills instead of luck when the results are favorable. But this portfolio was nothing more than a factor bet on the sector and good conditions in the market.

When the price of oil plummets and there are fewer credits available to small-cap companies, the portfolio would lose a lot of its value.

The main point of building a portfolio is to diversify the factor bets that we cannot forecast or control and concentrate our returns on the performance of individual businesses.

The Number of Holdings

Many successful investment firms are running portfolios that are considered as concentrated. For instance, the lucrative Berkshire Hathaway has several holdings that go beyond the 10 per cent of the overall value of its stock portfolio. The firm led by Warren Buffet invests with conviction behind the best stocks in the market.

Chances are, you don't have the resources, insights, and connections of a big investment firm to successfully run a concentrated investment portfolio.

As such, it is ideal for individual investors to spread their bets over a reasonable range of various stocks so you can avoid shooting yourself in the foot with stock investments that go wayward.

The fewer holdings you have, the bigger chance that your portfolio can deviate from the returns in the market. Hence, it is crucial to determine the right number of holdings you should have to maximize the benefits of diversification.

This institutional research went on to cite that as a general rule, company-specific (diversified) risk could be reduced by the following figures:

95% risk reduced when you hold 400 stocks

90% risk reduced when you hold 100 stocks

80% risk reduced when you hold 25 stocks

Another study was published in 2014 entitled "Equity Portfolio Diversification: How Many Stocks are Enough? Evidence from Five Developed Markets."

This research discovered that a higher number of stocks are required to diversify the risk during the financial downturn. In this kind of economic climate, the correlation between stocks is usually the highest.

In the US, the study concluded that to be certain of decreasing 90% of the risk, 90% of the time, the number of stocks required on average is around 55. This can however increase to around 110 stocks during times of economic turmoil.

With the findings from these studies, the sweet spot would seem in between 25 and 100 stocks. But if you throw in math into the mix, you should also consider factors that are unique to your financial constraints - trading cost, availability of resources and time for due diligence, and the size of your portfolio.

The effect of trading costs on your total returns will be bigger if your portfolio is smaller. If you have a small account, you may need to buy dividend ETFs instead of individual stocks so you can easily achieve diversification and save money on trading costs. You need less time in performing due diligence if you own more positions.

Although this is subjective, holding between 20 and 65 stocks can provide you a reasonable balance considering the factors of available time for due diligence, saving money from trading costs and the need to diversify.

Concentrating on higher quality stocks with a narrower range of possible outcomes can help in reducing risk to support a more focused portfolio. Meanwhile, a portfolio that is filled with risky stocks may choose a direction towards diversification with around 65 holdings.

Many individual investors prefer to roughly equate their positions because it can be difficult to know which holdings will perform well in the long run. Eventually, you have a unique opinion as an individual investor on how much diversification is sufficient and how much risk you can tolerate.

Diversification in the Industry Level

While adding more stocks in your portfolio can help you diversify the risk, there are still investors who end up with portfolios that are not well diversified because they follow strict investing rules (buying only stocks with P/E ratio less than 12x) or specific types of stocks (consumer products with household brands).

But holding on several stocks with the same characteristics will not help you maximize the benefits of diversification. This is due to the fact that stocks from similar industries are usually sensitive to the same factors and they usually have the same inherent risks.

Your investment portfolio could drastically underperform in the market when a shared factor like oil price or interest rates becomes unfavorable. Choosing stocks from various industries and sectors can help in diversifying the risk because if some industries are struggling, others might be doing well.

Many savvy dividend investors prefer to invest no more than 25% of their portfolio into a single sector, and try to own company stocks with minimum overlap into their actual operations.

There's no surefire way to determine which areas of the market would come in or out of favor, so sector diversification is crucial. But sector diversification must not come at the expense of contradicting principles of valuation or reaching beyond your comfort zone.

Consumer staples account for around 7% of the S&P500, but it doesn't mean you should buy stocks from this sector if you can't find one that is priced attractively. Moreover, you must not diversify into an industry or sector that is outside your circle of competence.

For instance, many conservative dividend investors have few investments in the technology sector because it evolves at a fast pace. It can be challenging to predict which companies will still be relevant for the next several years.

The takeaway here is that you must be deliberate with your diversification across business models and sectors. You still need to think through your investments. Choose market sectors that you are comfortable with and carefully evaluate each possible dividend investment as you gear towards diversification.

Financial Leverage

Using financial leverage for your investment portfolio can help you magnify your returns. This is one of the important factors that you need to understand when you are looking for safe stocks. The higher the debt volume of the company, the higher the stock price may fluctuate depending on the economic and business climate.

Hence, companies with huge debt loads and are naturally cyclical often have more volatile stocks. Some of the highly leveraged, lower quality may struggle if interest rates suddenly rise and credit conditions become stricter.

In building a portfolio, it is crucial to be aware of the general credit quality of your holdings. For many forms of investments, it is ideal to see an investment grade credit rating, strong coverage ratios, and no more than 50 per cent free cash flow generation.

Size of Investment

Historically, businesses with small market caps have shown better share price volatility compared to businesses with large market caps. Large companies are more liquid because of the availability of buyers and sellers.

If you enter into an order to sell or buy stocks of Apple, there should be someone on the other side of the counter who will agree to your asking price for the trade to proceed.

Companies with smaller market caps ($2 billion and under) could have much less liquidity in comparison to big cap companies. With fewer trades in the market, it is often difficult to move in and out of positions. Also, the spread between the buyer and the seller could become quite wide.

With less active trading liquidity, companies with small caps can easily outperform or underperform big cap stocks in various market settings. Small cap stocks also have high volatility because their businesses are usually less diversified compared to big caps.

Time Horizon and Price Volatility

Aside from the four risk factors discussed above, you should also understand price volatility or beta. This will help you take advantage of their long-term holding periods so you can enhance your dividend portfolios.

Beta will help you measure the volatility of the stock price to the market. By default, the market has a 1.0 beta, and individual stocks are ranked based on how much they deviate from the market in general.

Stocks with beta of more than 1.0 swings more than the market over time. When a stock has moved below the market, the beta of the stock is lower than 1.0.

The risk factors discussed above largely affects the beta of the stock. Smaller companies with less predictable business models and high volume of financial leverage will normally have higher betas.

It is crucial for investors to understand the different emotional tendencies and risk tolerances despite the fact that beta is backward-looking.

An investment portfolio filled with stocks that have beta values higher than 1.0 will likely move a lot compared to a portfolio that is filled with stocks with low beta.

You should also take note that beta is based on near-term price volatility that is not usually affected by business fundamentals. To put it simply, for long-term investors, a low or high beta does not indicate if an investment will be profitable over the next five years.

One advantage of individual investors is the capacity to hold stocks for a longer duration to allow strong underlying fundamentals to be reflected in the price of the stock. Building your dividend investment portfolio follows a slower pace.

Basically, it is ideal to own shares of high-quality growth stocks at a reasonable price than to stay on the sidelines trying to beat the quarterly profits game or time the market. The time horizon should be on your side and not against you.

Rebalancing your portfolio

As investors maintain a dividend portfolio, it is also important to occasionally rebalance that portfolio. This process gives the investor a chance to sell their shares at the higher points and then buy a stock when it's lower and has the potential to have a steady growth. This is often done in the world of index investments and can provide the same benefits for those with dividend payments.

Being able to rebalance a dividend portfolio can be an extremely useful way to remove the emotions an investor may have when they make their decisions regarding the ups and the downs of those holdings. Successful investing comes from making smart and diverse decisions that are meant for the long haul. Meaning, as an investor, you have to be diligent, patient, and willing to stick to your plan rather than look for quick cash.

Establish Your Targets

First, you have to start with a list of targets of what you would like in your dividend portfolio. Having these targeted sectors usually works the best, especially if you are an investor who wants to have up to thirty or more different stocks. While it can be hard to target each individual stock, it's better to focus on each industry and then base your individual decisions on their performance afterward.

How many you select in each sector is up to you as an investor. Sometimes you want to invest in ten different companies, and sometimes, you only find one or two. It all depends on how comfortable the investor is with that industry. But at the same time, it's important not to put all of the eggs in one basket. You need a diverse dividend portfolio for the best investment success.

For example, you decide that your portfolio will have the following sectors represented: financial (15 percent), utilities (15), telecommunications (15), energy (10), health care (10), housing (10), retail goods (10), technology (5), public transport (5), and bonds (5).

This would be a person who knows that there is a dependable growth in companies like financial institutions, like banks, utilities that provide to the public, and also telecommunications because of the growing need for mobile technology. The rest are of interest to this hypothetical investor but while playing it safe because they feel their bigger cuts have the best chance to bring consistent gains.

Select a Rebalancing Trigger

While some investors use a once-a-year trigger, many investors usually prefer to look at the different stocks in their portfolio more often than an annual checkup—many experts will recommend at least once every quarter, if not more. That's because there are so many fees that are linked with selling and buying that you wouldn't want to miss the opportunity to do either and cost yourself some big money.

Giving yourself about three months to make a move is generally acceptable because you don't necessarily want to be too hasty in case a company that had one minor dip one month could bounce back the next. There's an old expression that goes "Sell in May and go away"—which is like a warning to sell stocks in the month of May in order to avoid a potential seasonal decline that occurs in the market before returning in the full swing in November when numbers begin to go up again.

Another trigger that many investors use is establishing a percentage variation for each sector that can decide the rebalancing of your dividend portfolio. If your target is to have 10 percent in transportation, you could move it 3 percent one way or the other, and at that point, you could choose to sell or buy shares in that sector. The challenge comes from not just adjusting one sector but having to adjust the other six you own. Some experts recommend using the option to sell for the cash or invest additional funds.

Decide How You Will Rebalance Your Portfolio

Rebalancing a dividend portfolio doesn't mean that the investor has to sell stocks. Sometimes, it's just easier to only add funds as a matter of planning how to rebalance the percentages among the sectors in a portfolio.

An investor usually wouldn't sell ten stocks that are worth $100 and then pay the $10 commission fee because it just doesn't make much sense. Rebalancing your dividend portfolio might not be possible in an efficient manner and requires a large amount of planning before any type of decision is made. Remember, working with a dividend investment portfolio means no hasty decisions.

Let's say this hypothetical portfolio we have mentioned earlier is worth more than $100,000, and most of the investments have at least $5,000. Trades are made worth $1,000. That makes the aforementioned commission fee look really small in comparison—that's considering the 10–20 percent differential target within your portfolio.

Do So Within Each Sector

Keep an eye on each of the sectors represented in your dividend portfolio and analyze whether anything needs to be changed internally and not as much on a broad scale. If you own stocks in six banks under the financial sector, there might be an opportunity to rebalance between a few of them based on when you bought the stocks.

Eventually, the stocks that are doing well will need to be sold for a profit that can then be reinvested in the other existing banks in your portfolio. Or you could add a couple of other companies that have shown some great potential for making your portfolio even stronger. Usually, when an investor makes this type of decision, they are putting their money in a bank that is providing stronger and more consistent yields as opposed to one in their portfolio that wasn't pulling its weight.

Some experts would recommend waiting until the stock has reached a certain point above the original purchasing price—like around the 20 to 25 percent point. Then an investor is recommended to evaluate the time needed to build that profit and compare it to the other stocks in the portfolio.

Define Your Investing Rate

The first step is to fuel your dividend portfolio to really grow the snowball. Putting a sum at the start and then only using the dividend distributions to buy more stocks will grow your portfolio, but if you are starting small like I did, it will take you a while to reach your goals of financial independence and have enough investment income to cover your personal needs.

What you need to do is really to set aside a fix percentage or amount of your income (salary, business income, pension, etc.) for investments. For example, I put aside every month at least 40 percent of my overall income to be invested.

This will allow you to constantly fuel your portfolio and to buy new stocks or to add more stocks to a position you are already holding.

Diversify

Warren Buffett once said that diversifying your investments is only for people who don't know what they are doing. This might be true for somebody with a solid experience in the stock market, but if you're the average investor like me looking for financial independence, I won't suggest following his advice.

Instead, as you are building your portfolio, diversify. It doesn't mean buying good investments to make up for bad ones. It really means investing in several good dividend growth stocks to limit your risks if one of them goes south for some unexpected reason.

For example, the successful dividend investor Jason Fieber currently has over seventy dividend growth stocks in his portfolio. There is no set rule for diversification, but I recommend investing in fields that you are comfortable with.

For example, having a background as an engineer, I feel confident investing in technology companies, like IBM or Qualcomm, whereas, I am not so comfortable investing in insurance businesses as I know nothing about this field.

Reinvest Your Gains and Balance Your Global Portfolio

The last step you have to take is to reinvest your gains in order to get a nice compounding effect on your portfolio. Some brokerage firms even have an option to automatically buy more stocks using the dividend distributions.

This is the time to ensure your portfolio is rebalanced, for example, if one stock or category of stocks is starting to get a too large position in your portfolio.

However, even if this book is about dividend growth investing, I don't recommend investing all your money in dividend-paying stocks. You should rather consider dividend growth investing as part of a larger investment portfolio and diversify amongst several asset classes.

For example, in my own global investment portfolio, I usually aim of 35 percent of dividend growth stocks—the rest being made of peer-to-peer lending investments, real estate, bitcoin, and other investments.

Growth stocks

When choosing an investment to add to your long-term portfolio, you need to consider various factors. As a DIY investor, you should always strive to look for a dividend growth stock that matches specific requirements that make a stock 'a suitable investment.'

Like most people, you can start the process with a software tool that helps you to screen the thousands of stocks we have today. This option is relatively straightforward since all you need is to set a couple of filters on the software and have it sort things out for you.

The one thing you need to know about dividend investing is that the real work begins after you get your list of stocks from your preferred software tool. After you get this list, you need to conduct a detailed analysis of the companies so that you can narrow down to a handful.

Value stocks

Investors are always looking to create a value by investing in stocks that are undervalued, but these stocks have the potential to generate higher returns for investors in the future. Underestimated organizations can regularly give long haul benefits to the individuals who get their work done. It's a challenge to locate stocks or shares trading below their real value, but traders can use few ratios that can suggest how undervalued the stock is. For example, investors can use price to earnings and price to sales ratios. The lower ratio with respect to industry averages represents that the stock is undervalued. On the other hand, higher ratios show the stock is overvalued. In addition to these ratios, investors should also focus the future prospects of the stock to predict the upside potential.

Value stocks are regularly considered to convey less hazard than growth stocks since they are generally found with bigger, more-settled organizations. For instance, McDonald's was trading close to $90 a share in 2013, and analysts were expecting it to reach close to $100 a share by the end of the years. On the back of strong outlook, the stock hit almost $100 a share in the mid of that year. Technology industry has generated massive gains this year and had created significant value for investors. Stocks like Alphabet, NVIDIA, Ali Baba, are among the biggest gainers this year.

101

Chapter 12: Building your portfolio

Choosing the right stock

The stocks that you have been able to help your portfolio, as well. These are much different than other financial investment types, and they are able to offer you a lot of aid when it concerns your portfolio. They can make the portfolio more varied and can ensure that you are doing things the proper way. It is always a really good idea to include some good stocks to the portfolio so that you can ensure that you are getting the most out of the experience when it comes to investing.

While it might be frustrating at first to add stocks to your portfolio, you should try your hardest to make sure that they are in there. Begin with stocks that are low risk-- or do not cost you a lot of cash-- so that you will not lose a ton of money on them and you will have the ability to profit from them when it comes to different circumstances. The options that are included with your stocks should be quality and ought to be able to offer you with a lot of different chances.

Getting the most from your money

Every once in a while a company might decide to do a 2 for 1 stock split. This means that a company is dividing the number of stocks they have outstanding. If a company's stock price was $110 and it had $1 million shares outstanding after a 2-1 split the stock price would be $55 and there are now $2 million shares.

Companies do this when their stock price becomes too high. This might scare investors in purchasing such a high stock price. After a 2-1 split, the share of the company looks more affordable. Another reason is for **liquidity**, which means the ease of selling and buying of the stock.

If there are more shares on the market at a cheaper price, it makes the stock more liquid.

If you are an investor who owns the stock, a 2-1 split will give you double the number of shares. So if you had 30 stocks, a 2-1 will give you 30 extra for a total of 60 stocks. The price of the stock and your dividends are halved, but totaling up your shares will give you the same dividend amount and share amount you had before the 2-1 split.

Gaining shares

Since dividends are irreversible, your payments will forever generate cash in your books and business accounts. Therefore, the payment of dividends has an impact on the share price - it increases approximately when announcing the amount of the dividend declared and decreased by a similar amount at the opening date of the exit date.

Suppose a company trades at $60 per share and declares a dividend of $2 at the date of the announcement. Once the news is made public, the stock price will increase by approximately $2 to $62. Suppose the stock trades at $63 on a business day before the previous date. On the expiry date, it will be reduced by $2 similarly, and trading will start at $61 at the beginning of trading because anyone who buys on the expiry date will not receive the dividend.

How to reduce the risk of high-income share hangovers

Many people, including retirees, use stock dividends to increase their income. They face two main risks: their income could be affected by the reduction in dividends, and stock prices could fall due to changes in the economic scenario. How can you protect yourself against these dangers?

Another way to check the sustainability of dividends is to analyze the number of dividends on the company's profits that are paid to shareholders. If 90% of the profits go to investors, the risk of a fall in the profit on the dividend is much greater than if the value was 50%. Investors often use this figure of 50% - in other words, a "dividend hedge" of two - as a general rule for a secure dividend.

Watch for bond-like shares

Even when a dividend seems safe, the stock price may fall due to the changing economic situation.

Few professional investors doubt that bond prices will suffer as interest rates start to rise as liquidity becomes a more attractive competitor for bonds. This concerns equity investors because some stocks behave like bonds. Bond stocks are those with stable dividends and few prospects for growth, as are often found in the telecommunications, real estate and utility sectors, said Jacob de Tusch-Lec, Artemis Global Fund Manager.

So look for growth

Stocks of companies offering growth prospects are less likely to be dragged down by a slowdown in the bond market. These companies will not generally have the highest incomes. Investec fund analyst Andrew Summers said historical data showed that companies with returns between 60% and 80% of the highest rates in the market had the highest overall return. "This clearly shows how good it is to focus on performance, but also, high-yield companies are not good distributors of total return," he said.

JP Morgan US Equity Income's Fiona Harris said middle-dividend stocks were the "sweet spot." "Investors looking for quality companies with prudent management,

104

sustainable earnings, and strong dividend growth potential should do better than those who want to pay high dividends. About 75% of my fund is invested in stocks with returns ranging from 2% to 4%, "she said.

And get the balance right

Mr. de Tusch-Lec does not sell all his shares in bonds because no one knows when interest rates will start to rise. "I have to cover my bets on what happens to monetary policy," he said.

However, it has sold Unilever, Diageo and Nestle, because they have become too expensive and have "cheap" shares with high returns - like the Spanish utilities that produce 6 to 7 pc and whose market value does not, is only nine times higher - mixed with shares who report less but offer growth prospects.

"I have relatively large holdings in European companies because they offer income at a reasonable price," he said. "Then I found a good combination of revenue and growth at companies like AbbVie, a relatively unknown American biotech and pharmaceutical company, which provides 3.5%, in addition to a two-year annual growth. numbers. "

Chapter 13: Using options for Income

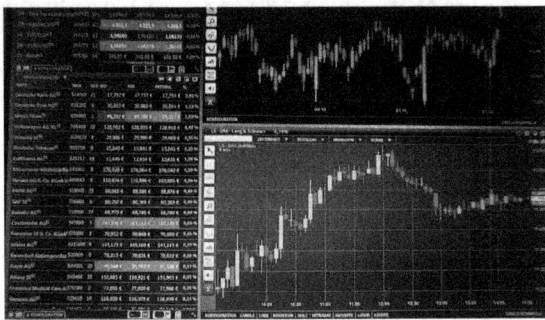

What are options

Dividends aren't the only way to earn money off the shares of stock you own. You can also earn money writing options contracts if you're not averse to the higher level of risk. In truth, the risk is relatively low and you can derive a solid income from selling options contracts. What's more, you could combine options with your other means of investing to increase your income potential. For example, you could invest in a stock that paid a solid dividend and reinvests the dividends as time goes on. But you could still make cash from the shares by writing covered call options on them. However, you have to be aware that there is a risk you would have to sell the shares. The real risk is relatively low for two reasons, however. The first is that few call options are actually exercised, and the second is that even if you're forced to sell your shares, you will still probably make a profit and can reinvest the proceeds from the sale in another stock.

No matter what we do or the precautions we take, there will always be risks in our life. Some of the risks we run into, however, can be guarded against through insurance. Defending against these risks is an essential part of creating a robust retirement plan. One thing that everyone should have is a form of auto and home insurance. If you have a relatively high net worth, it may be beneficial to add a form of umbrella policy on top of your existing insurance policies. Umbrella policies add an extra layer of insurance by allowing you to have additional liability protection. An example of an umbrella policy coming into play is shown in a scenario that happened to one couple, who we shall refer to as Frank and Elsa. This couple decided to retire in their 60s, and lived in a home with a pool. They were fond of hosting friends and often had parties in their home. One unfortunate evening, one of their guests accidentally fell into the pool, landing in a manner that left her paralyzed and the medical bills of their guest cost millions. Fortunately, the couple had added an umbrella policy that allowed them to protect their retirement assets from being consumed by the aftereffects of the unfortunate incident. Their umbrella policy covered one million dollars ($1,000,000) of the cost, in addition to the five hundred thousand ($500,000) paid out by their homeowner's policy. An insurance agent will be the one best equipped to assist you in choosing the right policy for you in order to protect your assets.

Another hotly discussed issue is life insurance. Many often wonder if they still need life insurance, and if they do get it, what kind or what extent of coverage they should get. Life insurance serves three purposes, each aligned to the different stages of our lives.

The first one is when we are still young, as life insurance helps to ensure that our spouse and children will have some measure of protection if we pass away too early. The second purpose arrives in middle age, ensuring that our spouse or young children will have a comfortable financial situation if you pass away early in your retirement years. The third and last purpose is if we reach old age and this type of insurance ensures that we can leave a financial legacy behind. The best time to decide on life insurance is before you retire. One way of determining the best option is to imagine the aftereffects of your passing, and what situation your spouse and other dependents will be left in. Once you pass, they will lose your salary or your social security benefits, or your pension. Getting life insurance is a way to protect and remedy the income gap that will arise after you pass. Some life insurance policies are permanent and may evolve over time. You may initially get them as protection for your retirement, and they may eventually be turned into ensuring your financial legacy. It also goes without saying that the costs of such insurance should be accounted for in your budget. There are many different kinds of insurance that one can get in order to ensure different levels of coverage, too many to be discussed here. It is best to discuss options with your financial advisor in order to find the best coverage for you to achieve these goals. You should also ensure that you minimize unnecessary coverage, as stopping payment of the premiums on these policies may allow for some extra funds during your retirement. One last thing that should be mentioned is disability insurance. This type of insurance is most crucial during your youth and middle age when you are actively working. After all, your best asset is your capability to earn, and you have to protect against anything happening to it. After you retire, this becomes of less importance, as there is much less income generation that has to be protected. In fact, most disability policies do not pay out if you are disabled when unemployed. This policy, therefore, is important while you are working, but becomes useless once you retire. In summary, you should plan your insurance to shore up weaknesses in your retirement plan, and mitigate risks. Talk to your insurance agent and financial planner to find the best form and amount of coverage that will serve the goals of your retirement plan.

What is a call option

A call option is an option to buy shares of stock at a fixed price. We call the fixed price the strike price. An option comes with an expiration date, and there is a wide range of expiration dates, but typically, they are going to expire in the near term like 3 weeks or a month. Underlying any options contract are shares of stock, and there are 100 shares of stock for each option contract.

Options contracts trade on exchanges that are set up specifically just for them, so there is an entire world of options traders living off the stock market. This works to your advantage. The reason is that most options traders are interested in profiting off the trading of the options contracts themselves, but they aren't really that interested in owning the shares of stock. But be aware that some people who buy options contracts are interested in buying the shares, so you may end up having to sell your shares in some circumstances. However, the data shows this doesn't happen most of the time, and so as we'll see, this provides an opportunity to earn a monthly income from your shares.

How to trade options for a living

First, you should familiarize yourself with some options in the marketplace so that you know how they are priced and you can get an idea of how much money you can make off your shares. To write an options contract, you will need to own at least 100 shares of the underlying stock. The price of the option is going to vary on two things; it will vary on the price of the underlying stock itself, but remember that the option also has an expiration date. So, the price of the option is also going to be impacted by the expiration date. The closer you get to the expiration date, the lower the price of the option – all other things being equal. A few days out from the expiration date, the price of the option is no longer impacted by the time left until the option expires. We call the decline in price from the time until the option expires time decay, and the value that goes into the option from the amount of time left on the contract is called the extrinsic value.

The value of the option that comes from the underlying stock is called the intrinsic value. Ideally, the intrinsic value would come directly from the price of the underlying shares. Remember, there are 100 shares for an option contract, so a rise in the price of the underlying share price by $ 1 would mean a $ 100 rise in the price of the option. Similarly, a $ 1 drop in the share price would mean a drop in the price of the option by $ 100.

In the real world, the relationship isn't that cut and dry, but there is a number that you can look at in stock data that will give you a good estimate of how the price of the option will change with changes in the underlying share price. This is a Greek symbol called delta. It's a number that ranges between 0.0 and 1.0, so if Delta is 1.0, then the change in the price of the option will be ideal that is a $ 1 rise in share price will result in a $ 100 rise in the price of the option. If Delta was 0.7, then the price of the option would rise to $ 70 for every $ 1 rise in the price of the stock.

The idea of a call option is to give a bullish investor, that is someone who is expecting the stock price of some investment to rise in the near term, the ability to buy shares of stock at a cheaper price that is agreed upon beforehand. So say that you own 100 shares of a stock that is trading at $ 100. Maybe a bullish investor out there believes that the stock price is going to rise to $ 105 a share. But they want a bargain and they're only willing to pay $ 102 a share. So, they can buy a call option with that strike price. If at any time that the call option hasn't expired, the share price goes above $ 102 a share, that would mean that the buyer of the option could exercise their rights to buy the shares. And the seller of the shares would be obligated to sell them at the discounted price of $ 102.

Now, let's look at it from the seller's perspective. You may be bullish on the stock over the long term, but you may not believe it will pass $ 102 a share. Also, chances are you bought the stock back in the past for a lower price than it's currently trading at. Therefore, if you had to sell the shares at $ 102, you wouldn't be too bothered, since you would probably be making a profit anyway – even though that profit might be quite a bit lower than the profit that you would have made selling them at $ 105 a share. However, as we'll see in a second, some of that difference is going to be covered by the money you get by selling the option. An option isn't free. Someone that wants one has to buy it. Prices are quoted on a per-share basis. So, if you look up options prices, you will need to multiply the quoted price by 100 to get the price someone would actually have to pay. Let's look at our favorite dividend stock, Abbvie.

The share price at this instant is $ 75.70. There are call options with strikes above and below this share price. For a call option, when the market price of the share goes above the strike price for the call option, the price of the option goes up by a lot. Options with prices above the current share price are still worth money (until they expire), but the higher you go in strike price above the current market price, the lower the cost of the option.

So, we see a call option expiring in three weeks that has a strike price of $ 76.50, or $ 0.80 above the share price. It's estimated that there is a 69.7% chance of profit, meaning that before the option expires, the share price has a 69.7% chance of being lower than the strike price of $ 76.50. The price is quoted as $ 1.40.

So, if you owned 100 shares of Abbvie, you could sell this option for $ 1.40. Since the contract covers 100 shares, you can sell a contract on 100 shares for $ 1.40 x 100 = $ 140. If you own 1,000 shares, you can, therefore, sell ten contracts and earn $ 1,140. The payment for an options contract is called the premium. So, the premium is money you earn off the stock, and odds are you will be able to take the money as profit and still keep your shares. But be aware there is a risk that if the stock price went up to $ 77 a share, which would put your price below the market price, you might have to sell your shares for $ 76.50.

You can reduce your risk by picking a call option with an even higher strike price, making it less likely that you'll have to sell your shares because the probability of the stock price reaching the strike price and exceeding it gets smaller with each higher strike price you consider. Remember, options expire, with most of them expiring in the near term. That means it's likely the three or four weeks will pass and you'll still have your shares. Especially with a stock like Abbvie that isn't all that volatile.

So, let's suppose that the price did go to $ 77 and you had to sell your shares for $ 76.50. In fact, let's suppose it goes to $ 78.50 so that you would lose out on $ 2 a share. First of all, note that you probably aren't losing anything, what you are losing is potential

109

profits. If you had purchased the shares in the past, say in June of 2017, you paid $ 67 a share for them. So, even though you can't sell them for $ 78.50, you're still selling them at a higher price than you paid for the shares. Plus the money earned from selling the options contract is yours to keep. So, you've made $ 1.40 per share from that, and so, you're nearly at the $ 78.50 price when you add all that up.

In the jargon of options traders, a call option is in the money if the market price of the stock goes above the strike price of the options contract. If you are buying and selling shares looking for capital gains, then this scenario isn't going to bother you at all. However, if you are a dividend investor, you do have that risk staring at you that you will lose the shares and so be out the dividend.

But the fact is most options traders are looking to make profits buying and selling the options contracts themselves. Therefore, they are probably going to end up selling an options contract to someone else if the option goes in the money. Why would they do that rather than buying the shares? Because an options contract that is in the money is worth more, and so they can sell it and take their profits.

Let's look at some prices of the money call options for AbbVie that expire on the same day. A $ 75 call is priced at $ 2.21, so it would sell for $ 221. A $ 73 call is priced at $ 3.58, so it would sell for $ 358. That would mean if you had 1,000 shares, you could sell 10 options contracts for $ 3,580. That isn't a bad passive monthly income.

Dividend Stocks aren't volatile

One of the good things about dividend stocks when it comes to this strategy is they don't tend to be volatile. A volatile stock that has wild price swings is more likely to exceed the strike price, which might cause you to have to sell your shares. Since most dividend stocks are slow and steady as they go, growing but doing so at a slower and steadier clip as opposed to say, Tesla, Netflix, and Amazon, you're less likely to face the prospect of having to sell your shares.

However, the risk that you will have to do so is real, and sometimes, it will happen. So, be sure to pick a strike price that you are willing to live with, so if you are not comfortable selling the shares at $ 76.50, pick $ 77 or whatever suits you. Just remember the higher the strike price the less money you're going to earn. The further out you go, the more money you make Calls that expire months in the future can be sold for high premiums. Looking out six months for AbbVie, we see that a $ 77.50 call sells for $ 4.73 per share, so 100 shares per option mean we could sell one option contract for $ 473. If we owned 1,000 shares, then we could sell 10 contracts for $ 4,730.

You can go even further out in time. If an option expires more than nine months into the future, it's considered a LEAP. That stands for Long term Equity Anticipation Security. For AbbVie, we can check a year and a half into the future and see that a $ 70 call is selling for $ 11.28, so the price of the options contract is 100 x $ 11.28 = $ 1,128. Just remember that the longer you have until option expiration, the more chance there is that someone might "call" the option and force you to sell your shares. So, you should choose a strike price that would be above the price you paid for the shares when you bought them.

Put Options

We can use put options to mitigate the risk of having to sell our shares with the covered call option, but first, let's get a little bit of familiarity with what put options are. A put option gives the buyer the option to buy shares of stock at a particular price. Like a call option, that price is called the strike price. One way that options traders use this to make money is they buy a put option for a stock that they think is going to go way down. Then, if the stock does go down, they buy 100 shares at the cheap market price, and then they exercise the option and sell them to the writer of the contract at the strike price. The profit is the difference between the strike price and the market price. Let's use an example.

Suppose that a stock is trading at $ 100 a share. You buy a put option with a strike price of $ 90 a share, but you don't own the stock. But you're basically shorting it; you would do this if you think the stock is in for a massive decline. Suppose that the option sold for $ 2, which would be a total price of $ 200. Suppose that the stock does decline significantly before the expiration date of the option. For the sake of illustration, imagine that it drops to $ 40 a share. So you buy 100 shares for $ 40 x 100 = $ 4,000.

But since you own a put option with a $ 90 strike price, you can exercise it. That means you can sell the shares for $ 90 a share. So you make $ 90 x 100 = $ 9,000. Your profit is $ 5,000 from the sale of the shares. You also had to pay a premium for the put option, which was $ 200. So your total profit is $ 4,800.

Selling in the money call options

So, we see one way that someone might profit from a decline in stock price, but there is a way you can profit from a decline in stock price using covered calls as well. This is done by selling a call that is already in the money. So, let's say that for the sake of argument, there is going to be bad news coming out in 3 weeks about AbbVie. Anticipating that the stock price will drop, and so make a call option that is out of the money worthless, you write a call option but one that is in the money now, so you can charge a higher premium. So, if the current market price is $ 75.70, you can sell a call option for $ 74 if you expect the share price to drop below that. The price for that option is $ 2.85 x 100 shares = $ 285. Again, if you had 1,000 shares, that means you could make $ 2850. If the share price doesn't end up dropping, you might be forced to sell your shares, so choose a share price that you are comfortable with. If it does drop below the strike price, then you keep your shares and made $ 2,850 from the sale of the option premium.

Climbing the dividend ladder

As investors maintain a dividend portfolio, it is also important to occasionally rebalance that portfolio. This process gives the investor a chance to sell their shares at the higher points and then buy a stock when it's lower and has the potential to have a steady growth. This is often done in the world of index investments and can provide the same benefits for those with dividend payments.

Being able to rebalance a dividend portfolio can be an extremely useful way to remove the emotions an investor may have when they make their decisions regarding the ups and the downs of those holdings. Successful investing comes from making smart and diverse decisions that are meant for the long haul. Meaning, as an investor, you have to be diligent, patient, and willing to stick to your plan rather than look for quick cash.

Establish Your Targets

First, you have to start with a list of targets you would like in your dividend portfolio. Having these targeted sectors usually works the best, especially if you are an investor who wants to have up to thirty or more different stocks. While it can be hard to target each stock, it's better to focus on each industry and then base your own decisions on their performance afterward.

How many you select in each sector is up to you as an investor. Sometimes you want to invest in ten different companies, and sometimes, you only find one or two. It all depends on how comfortable the investor is with that industry. But at the same time, it's important not to put all of the eggs in one basket. You need a diverse dividend portfolio for the best investment success.

For example, you decide that your portfolio will have the following sectors represented: financial (15 percent), utilities (15), telecommunications (15), energy (10), health care (10), housing (10), retail goods (10), technology (5), public transport (5), and bonds (5).

The owner of such a diverse portfolio would be a person who knows that there is a dependable growth in companies like financial institutions, banks, utilities that provide to the public, and also telecommunications because of the growing need for mobile technology. The rest are of interest to this hypothetical investor while still playing it safe because they feel their bigger cuts have the best chance to bring consistent gains.

Select a Rebalancing Trigger

While some investors use a once-a-year trigger, many investors usually prefer to look at the different stocks in their portfolio more often than an annual checkup—many experts will recommend at least once every quarter, if not more. That's because there are so many fees that are linked with selling and buying, that you wouldn't want to miss the opportunity to do either and cost yourself some big money.

Giving yourself about three months to make a move is generally acceptable because you don't necessarily want to be too hasty in case a company that had one minor dip one month could bounce back the next. There's an old expression that goes, "Sell in May and go away"—which is like a warning to sell stocks in the month of May. It is recommended in order to avoid a potential seasonal decline that occurs in the market, before returning in full swing in November, when numbers begin to go up again.

Another trigger that many investors use is establishing a percentage variation for each sector that can decide the rebalancing of your dividend portfolio. If your target is to have 10 percent in transportation, you could move it 3 percent one way or the other, and at that point, you could choose to sell or buy shares in that sector. The challenge comes from not just adjusting one sector but having to adjust the other six you own. Some experts recommend using the option to sell for the cash or invest additional funds.

Decide How You Will Rebalance Your Portfolio

Rebalancing a dividend portfolio doesn't mean that the investor has to sell stocks. Sometimes, it's just easier to only add funds as a matter of planning how to rebalance the percentages among the sectors in a portfolio.

An investor usually wouldn't sell ten stocks that are worth $100 and then pay the $10 commission fee because it doesn't make much sense. Rebalancing your dividend portfolio might not be possible in an efficient manner and requires a large amount of planning before any type of decision is made. Remember, working with a dividend investment portfolio means no hasty decisions.

Let's say this hypothetical portfolio we have mentioned earlier is worth more than $100,000, and most of the investments have at least $5,000. Trades are made worth $1,000. That makes the aforementioned commission fee look really small in comparison—that's considering the 10–20 percent differential target within your portfolio.

Do So Within Each Sector

Keep an eye on each of the sectors represented in your dividend portfolio and analyze whether anything needs to be changed internally and not as much on a broad scale. If you own stocks in six banks under the financial sector, there might be an opportunity to rebalance between a few of them, based on when you bought the stocks.

Eventually, the stocks that are doing well will need to be sold for a profit that can then be reinvested in the other existing banks in your portfolio. Or you could add a couple of other companies that have shown some great potential for making your portfolio even stronger. Usually, when an investor makes this type of decision, they are putting their money in a bank that is providing stronger and more consistent yields as opposed to one in their portfolio that wasn't pulling its weight.

Some experts would recommend waiting until the stock has reached a certain point above the original purchasing price—like around the 20 to 25 percent point. Then an investor is recommended to evaluate the time needed to build that profit and compare it to the other stocks in the portfolio.

Define Your Investing Rate

The first step is to fuel your dividend portfolio to really grow the snowball. Putting a sum at the start and then only using the dividend distributions to buy more stocks will grow your portfolio. However, if you are starting small like I did, it will take you a while to reach your goals of financial independence and have enough investment income to cover your personal needs.

What you need to do is set aside a fix percentage or amount of your income (salary, business income, pension, etc.) for investments. For example, I put aside every month at least 40 percent of my overall income to be invested.

Doing this will allow you to constantly fuel your portfolio and to buy new stocks or to add more stocks to a position you are already holding.

Diversify

Warren Buffett once said that diversifying your investments is only for people who don't know what they are doing. This might be true for somebody with a solid experience in the stock market, but if you're the average investor like me looking for financial independence, I won't suggest following his advice.

Instead, as you are building your portfolio, diversify. It doesn't mean buying good investments to make up for bad ones. It really means investing in several good dividend growth stocks to limit your risks if one of them goes south for some unexpected reason.

For example, the successful dividend investor Jason Fieber currently has over seventy dividend growth stocks in his portfolio. There is no set rule for diversification, but I recommend investing in fields that you are comfortable with.

114

In my case, for example, having a background as an engineer makes me feel confident in investing in technology companies, like IBM or Qualcomm. However, I am not so comfortable investing in insurance businesses as I know nothing about this field.

Maintenance and growth

Now that you have learned how to make the best dividend investment in your entire portfolio, you will need to learn how to manage all of the wealth that you are going to have in the end. This may actually be the trickiest part of dividend investing and is often the part where everyone slips up and loses the money that they have made. It is best that you are prepared for your passive income and you are doing what you can to make sure that you are getting what you need out of it.

Save It

The easiest thing that you can do with the income that you get is to save it. It is a good idea to try to save around 50% of what you make from the passive income and this is easy to do, especially if you have not taken on investing full time. Save the money so that you will have it later on in case something happens or just for the sake of saving it. By doing this, you will give yourself a great start to a retirement, a vacation fund or something else that will make your life better.

It should be relatively easy to save the money that you have made with passive income. Since you don't have to worry about the problems that come with a traditional job, you will not need to worry about making money. You can also save a much larger amount of money if you are using the investment as supplemental income. If you are using the investment as your main source of income, it may be more difficult to save 50%, but there is still a chance that you will be able to do it.

High Interest

The best way to save your money is to find a high-interest savings account. This can be from your bank, online or even on a CD that will make you more money. The best things about high-interest savings accounts are that they are yet another form of passive income. You don't have to do anything other than put your money in the account and it will experience growth during that time. This is a great way to make even more money than what you already made on the investment.

The high-interest savings account will obviously not make you as much money as reinvesting it or even the initial investment, but it will help to keep it in your hands and grow a little bit more. The more money that you put into the account, the higher the interest will be because you will be able to make more money from what you were doing with it. It is a good idea to always find the highest rate possible and stick to it. You can always find out if the bank or institution where your money is at can raise the interest amount and in fact, some banks do that automatically if you keep your savings account open for a long time.

Spend It

If you have a plan to spend your dividend investment income, you will be less likely to spend it on things that you don't need. Set aside what you are going to spend out of the money that you make and ensure that you only spend that much. If you give yourself a set amount of money, you will be less likely to spend recklessly and make purchases that you may regret later on, after you have run out of the dividend payment.

It may seem counterintuitive, but you can even put aside money specifically that you can waste on things that you don't want. This is "blow" money that you can spend on anything – from new high heels to a gallon of ice cream at the grocery store. The money is yours to use in any way that you want and it will help you to budget it.

You will find that, the more money you make, the harder it is to budget. Keep a 10% rule for your "blow" money so that you can make sure you do not get out of hand with it and can keep it below your average spending amount. This will help to keep your spending in check.

Invest It

Investing the money that you have made from your initial investment is one of the easiest ways that you can grow the wealth that you have already made from dividend investing. The investment that you make does not need to be perfect, and it is something that you can feel good about. Any type of investment is better than nothing and putting your money back into investing is a great way to make even more money.

When you are going to reinvest the money that you have already made, there are two different ways that you can do it. You can make money and put it back into the investment that you already did, with the dividends. Or, you can choose to try something different in the investment world. By making sure that you know how to do each of these things, you will have plenty of options when it comes time to make more money from what you have already.

Try New Things

If you have money that you want to use and invest, but you do not want to do anymore dividend investing, you can always try to do a different type of investment. There are many different options that you can try out, but the majority of these will be profitable if you know how to put your money in the right place. Trying out an index fund or something similar will be an excellent way for you to make the most amount of money on top of what you have already made. You may also consider something like a REIT.

Switching it up and trying something different can change the portfolio that you have and give you the variety that you need to make sure that you are doing things the right way. It can be hard to guarantee that you get that variety, especially if you are focusing on dividend investments. However, investing some of the money back into something else is the easiest way for you to make sure that you are making the most money possible.

Your portfolio will thank you for the variety that you have added to it.

Put it Back In

Another option that you have when it comes to your investments is to put the money back into your dividend investment. You don't need to put all of your money back into the investment that you have already made, but it is a good idea to choose the right way to be able to invest if you are working towards doing more with what you have to offer.

If you are going to invest money back into your dividend investment, you need to make sure that you do it the right way. Do not invest all of your money into the same venture. This is dangerous and could leave you with no income. If you are able to invest money, you should do around 50% of the money that you have made. This is a good number because it will leave you feeling that you have made a good choice with keeping the money, as well as putting it back into the investment. You can also make a lot more money from investing 50% as opposed to 15% or 25%.

Chapter 14: Tax Implications

It is said that two things in life have absolute certainty: death and taxes.

When you are an investor, you have to be double-careful about your taxes, because each type of investment in your portfolio might be taxed differently.

Unfortunately, taxes are not one of the strong points of dividend investing. In fact, this type of investment is disadvantageous from two tax-related points of view.

The first one is connected to the fact that you will be double-taxed: once through the corporation tax applied to all the earnings made by a company (which will consequently lower the amount of money available for dividend payments) and the second time when you have to pay income tax on your received dividend payments.

Tax rates vary a lot from one investor to another, according to everyone's specific situation. In some cases, you might be able to legally reduce the taxes paid on dividends by using the so-called "tax-sheltered accounts" (IRAs, Roth IRAs, 401k accounts, and so on). It is, however, very important to discuss this with an accountant and see if this is your particular situation.

Furthermore, it is important to note that if a company does not pay its retained earnings in the form of dividends, they still have the option to buy back the shares you purchased from them. In this case, you might be better off selling the stock back than receiving dividends, because this way, you will not be paying as much in taxes. Again, however, this varies from one situation to another, so it is not a generally accepted rule of any kind.

The second tax-related disadvantage of owning dividend-paying stocks is connected to the fact that sometimes, these companies will tap investors. This usually happens when they need to raise cash (or when they want to raise fresh equity). When this happens, you might find yourself in a circling situation that makes you receive a dividend payment, and then you are asked by the company to pay cash in a rights issue. Consequently, you send the cash back to the company for further reinvestment, but you are faced with a tax wedge that is completely unnecessary.

Dividend-paying stocks are frequently associated with exchange-traded funds (also called ETFs). These funds collect the dividend payments on behalf of the investors, and then disburse them accordingly.

There are several disadvantages associated with this practice. On the one hand, these funds handle all the organizational matters of your investments, making it relatively easy for you to manage your portfolio.

On the other hand, this also means that ETFs will charge a fee for their services (which is normal, but not necessarily less annoying for investors who want to see higher profitability for their investments.

Furthermore, the timing of a dividend payment that goes through an EFT first might be delayed as well. Depending on the ex-dividend date, on the record date, and on the payment date set by the ETF you may or may not receive your dividend payments.

Different ETFs have different rules and fees, so it is quite important for you to analyze the ETF both from the point of view of the type of companies in it and from the point of view of the expense ratio (which shouldn't be higher than 0.50%).

Fees are quite unavoidable when it comes to dividend investing, but some ETFs might be better than others, for different people. This is why it is extremely important that you run an analysis that suits your particular situation and that you don't buy stock in a dividend-paying company just because you "heard" it's a good move.

Clearly, dividend investing shows a pretty good array of benefits. As mentioned before, one of the most important ones is the fact that this type of investment is frequently safer than others.

Unfortunately, "safe" is usually at the other end of the pole with "skyrocketing" - so you shouldn't expect your income to simply boom as a result of making dividend investments. Yes, they can definitely add to your portfolio, and yes, a collection of good dividend investment options can definitely help you boost your income.

However, you should not expect **The Wolf of Wall Street**-type of income growth.

Most of the dividends hold at about 2-3% in terms of yield. This means that if you invest $250,000, you will only see a maximum of $7,500 in dividend payments every year.

If your investment goal is retirement, that might amount to a considerable sum of money over the course of a couple of decades. However, it is important to know that the safest way to withdraw your investment money for retirement includes not touching the principal (the main investment you made).

If patience is your strong suit and you are using dividend investing in combination with other types of investment, the situation is far different, and dividends are a very good choice. Yet, if you are in a rush to make a fortune, this might not be the best solution for you.

119

Dividend investing is by no means an easy way out of financial worries. But then again, nothing is, except winning the lottery or accidentally striking a gold mine and buying a low-priced stock that will storm into a very good sale in a relatively short amount of time.

The absolute golden rule to successful investments is making sure you don't put all your eggs in one basket. This means that you should resort to a variety of types of investments in a variety of businesses and industries.

The remainder of this book is dedicated to helping you find those precise dividend investment options that provide you with all the advantages with the least of the disadvantages as possible. Of course, it is impossible to predict the future - but even so, there are certain strategies you can use to minimize the risk of your dividend investments and maximize their profitability.

It depends on a country's laws how it taxes or doesn't dividends. These laws change too. At some point dividends can be tax exempt, but if country stores up a lot of public debts it may start searching things it can tax and dividends can become one of them.

Another thing you should know is that countries typically sign double taxation treaties meaning that if you make dividends in one country, you only pay taxes on them in your home country in order to avoid being taxed in the country dividends originate and in the country they are paid to. You need to check your local laws and how it related to investment abroad if you are not a US citizen.

Double taxation idea (taxes paid in two countries) should not be confused with the idea of income being taxed and then dividends being taxed. That is also called double taxation. As most companies that have been paying dividends for long years are in US you should know how dividends were and are taxed in US. Below is the chart showing time periods and tax rates on dividends

Options trading

Introduction

Congratulations on purchasing *Options Trading Crash Course* and thank you for doing so.

Options trading represents an unprecedented opportunity. In this book you will learn how options trading allows you to use leverage to build income and wealth using small amounts of invested capital. Until recently, options have only been available to the pros, but now ordinary investors like you can get in the options game and start making profits. As we go along we will detail exactly how options work and how you can start making big profits trading options.

We will begin the book with a discussion of what options are and the basic mechanics of how they work. Then you will learn the practical steps that you need to take to start trading options.

After we get the basics out of the way, we will teach you how to earn profits. We'll begin by explaining the different types of stock options and how you can use them in order to make quick profits. We'll teach you what you need to look for in order to avoid losses and earn money, and then we'll explain the secrets the pros use to win on nearly every trade. Our discussion will pull back the curtain on all the important characteristics of options that are used by the experts, including the strike price, expiration date, how options are priced, and the fabled Greeks. We'll also cover the steps you need to take in order to build a successful trading plan and how to maintain a healthy trading psychology and state of mind that will help you avoid mistakes and earn profits.

With our foundations laid, we will cover the important trading strategies used by options traders to make money no matter which direction the stock market moves. Unlike stocks, with options you can make profits if the price goes up, goes down, or even stays the same. We'll show you exactly how, and we'll explain the exact strategies the experts use in order to earn big time profits.

Options trading seems mysterious but it's actually not as complicated as you've probably imagined. By the time you have completed this book you'll be ready to start making your first trades and earn the kinds of profits you've always dreamed of.

There are many different books on options trading that are available, thanks again for choosing this one! Every effort was made to ensure it is full of as much useful information as possible, please enjoy!

Day 1: An Overview of Options

If you want to make profits from the stock market, most people think in terms of buying a lot of shares and day or swing trading them. That can work, but the downside of trading stocks and earning short term profits is that you have to invest thousands of dollars – even tens of thousands of dollars, in order to make a profit of $200 or $500. What if there was a way to make a $200 profit in a single day on the stock market – only investing $100 or $200?

It turns out there is, and the way to do it is by trading options.

Options are a way to use leverage to earn big profits on the stock market. Leverage normally means using borrowed money in order to make profits, but in the case of options you use leverage in a completely novel way. An options contract gives you the control of one hundred shares of stock, and you can earn big profits on the price movements of that stock without actually owning it. That is true leverage!

What's more, as we'll see options allow you to make profits on the price movements of stock that are not possible when simply buying shares. For example, you can make money on options contracts in the same way that you would buying stock, that is if the share price of a given stock goes up, you earn a profit.

But, unless you are a big time player, that is the only way you can make profits on the price movements of stock – buying shares. It turns out that with options you can easily make profits on declining stock prices, even when you only invest a hundred or two hundred dollars.

Moreover, you can make profits on options if the price of the stock doesn't move at all. In this book we are going to show you the exact steps that you can take in order to earn profits from stock that isn't moving very much. Using a secret strategy called the iron

123

condor, you can make profits when the stock price stays the same or bounces around in between two fixed values.

We'll also show you how to earn money when a stock is positioned to make a large price move – but you have no idea which direction that price move is going to go. For example, stock can move big when there is an earnings call. However, before the call nobody knows if the company is going to report earnings that meet expectations or not. As an options trader, it won't matter – you can make profits either way. And we are going to show you how in this book.

Options also provide a way to earn a regular income. Dividend investors have to sink hundreds of thousands of dollars – at a minimum – to earn a decent income from their stocks. As an income generating device, options allow you to earn a solid middle class income using only a few thousand dollars. The problem is most people have no idea how to go about it – but we're going to give you the exact steps you need in order to make this happen.

But before we learn all the secrets behind options trading, we need to learn what options really are and how they work. That is the topic of this chapter and we'll be elaborating on this in more detail in the following chapters as well.

What are options
An option is a contract that gives you the right to buy or sell shares of stock at a fixed price. A single options contract is for 100 shares of stock. So, one options contract might give you the ability to sell a hundred shares of a stock at $100 a share, or it might give you the ability to buy 100 shares of stock at $100 a share. The price that is specified in the contract is fixed, and so it doesn't necessarily matter if the market price of the stock is fluctuating as far as that goes. That is, even if the stock price were to rise to say $200 a share, or even $300 a share, if you have an option that specifies that you have the right to buy 100 shares at $100 a share, that contract must be honored if you choose to exercise it.

Of course, you don't have to exercise it, and that is why they are called "options". It is optional for the buyer to actually exercise their rights under the contract and buy or sell the shares. In fact, many options traders never do so. As the market price of the stock goes up and down, the value of the option itself goes up and down and so there are opportunities to profit merely by trading the options contract itself. This happens on the options exchange. In fact, there are several options markets where options are traded, but as a trader working through a broker that is all hidden from you, and you simply buy or sell your options through the broker without worrying about where they are really traded and who buys or sells the options.

Options can earn profits for people buying or selling them. For this reason, many people enter into an options trade by "writing" or selling to open an options contract. These people, who sell an options contract to open their position in the market, have the highest risk. That is because if you sell to open an options contract you are legally obligated to follow through on that contract. So, if you have sold to open an option to sell 100 shares at a given price, if a buyer decides to exercise the contract, you have to sell them the shares. Likewise, there are certain types of options contracts that require you to purchase shares of stock at a fixed price. If it is profitable for the buyer to do so, they can exercise their rights and decide to sell you the shares, and you must buy them in that case.

That sounds pretty scary, and if you are careless it could get you into trouble. However, as we will see using sound strategies you can sell options at relatively low risk to yourself and earn an income doing so.

As a buyer, you have much lower risk. Your maximum risk is fixed. This is given by the price you pay for the option. In most cases, this is going to run from $30 or $50 up to a few hundred dollars, although options on highly priced stocks like Amazon might be pricier. A buyer is normally hoping to earn profits from the price movements of the stock. Since options are traded on their own markets, this means that the prices of options are fluctuating up and down as the price of the stock increase or drops down, and so you can purchase at a low price and sell high with the options without ever actually buying the stock that backs the option. Buyers of options contracts will use different strategies in order to earn profits, which we will talk about in later chapters.

Options Pricing and Expiration Dates

So, an option is a contract on the shares of a particular stock. That means you might buy an option on Apple, IBM, Boeing, or Facebook for example. However, there is something important you need to know about options. Options come with an expiration date. If an option expires, and you haven't exercised or sold the option, it becomes worthless.

This means that you need to keep a close eye on the expiration dates of any options that you invest in. In addition, you will need a specific plan that will help you decide when to get out of the options contract to either make a profit or to cut your losses.

Sellers need to be aware of expiration dates as well. If an option expires and it is "in the money", which means that it would be advantageous for a buyer to exercise their rights under the contract, then you will have to meet your obligations. That means either buying or selling 100 shares of stock. Most people that sell options get out of their obligation as the expiration date approaches so that they are not put into this position.

Either way, it is important for an options trader to be very aware of the expiration date of any option that they invest in.

Buying and Selling Options

As we mentioned earlier, you can buy to open an options contract, or you can sell to open an options contract. If an options contract is "in the money" this means that the option can be exercised by a buyer to earn a profit, which means either buying or selling 100 shares of stock. On the other hand, if it is "out of the money", then it would not be profitable for the buyer to exercise the option. Sellers of options contracts generally hope that the option will be out of the money. If a contract were to expire and it was out of the money, it is said to "expire worthless". Since the contract has expired without any value, the seller of the option pockets any money they received selling it, and they don't have to worry about buying or selling shares of stock.

A buyer of an option is normally a trader. That means they are hoping to sell it at a higher price than they paid for it. As the price of the stock goes up and down, it can cause the market price of any options contract on that stock to move up or down. This provides traders an opportunity to earn profits without actually investing in the stock. When the value of an option goes up, they can sell the option to another trader for a profit.

Keep in mind that if you buy an option to enter your investment position, you are not under any sort of obligation. In other words, if you later sell the option, you are not under the seller's obligation. Only the original seller of an option is required to either buy or sell shares of stock. So, you can buy an option, and if its value goes up you can sell it off and take a profit and walk away from it. Many people trade options without having any intention to own the shares of stock or trade shares of stock whatsoever. But if you want to, you can definitely buy or sell the shares if it becomes advantageous and you can afford it.

Advantages of Options

Options carry many advantages over trading stock. The first advantage is the amount of capital required to enter into a trade. If you want to buy 100 shares of a stock, and on the market it's priced at $200 a share, that means you must come up with $20,000. But with an option, you can control the underlying shares of stock only investing the small sum of money required to buy an option. For a stock trading at $200, depending on circumstances the price of an option could vary from $150 - $300. That is a lot less than having to come up with $20,000, and as we'll see you can earn huge profits from the price movements of the stock that the option represents without having to come up with huge amounts of capital. For that reason, options trading opens up large profit possibilities for small investors that they would not have otherwise.

Options also allow you to enter into complex trades that aren't possible when investing directly in stock. The advantages of this is that you can setup trades that allow you to earn profits with different types of stock movements. So, you can earn profits if the stock is moving up, if it is dropping, or if it is ranging which means it is staying within a narrow range of prices. You can also make profits if the share price of a stock shoots off in one direction or another. Later in the book we will show you how to set up different types of trades that let you deal with virtually any type of situation.

To summarize, options trading lets you get in the market with a small amount of upfront capital, it lets you leverage 100 shares of stock without actually owning it, and you can utilize trading strategies that stock traders are not able to use.

Options Terminology

When you enter into any specialized field, there is some terminology or jargon you need to become familiar with. Options trading is no different. We are going to expand on this as we go throughout the book, but here we will introduce you to the most fundamental terms used in the options trading markets.

Call Option

A call option is a specific type of contract that grants the buyer the right to buy 100 shares of stock at a fixed price. This important price is called the strike price. The strike price is fixed, and must be honored by the seller of the option. People buy call options when they think the price of a given company's stock (or an index fund) is going to rise.

Put Option

A put option is an option that provides the ability to sell shares of stock at a fixed price. This is also called the strike price. Put options also typically cover 100 shares. Like a call option, the strike price is not something that changes, it is part of the contract. A put option is good to buy if you believe that conditions are going to result in declining prices.

Exercising the Option

If you have a call option, if you decide to buy the 100 shares of stock at the strike price, you are exercising the option. If you have a put option, if it is profitable to do so, you can buy the shares on the stock market. Then, you could use the option by selling them to the originator of the put option. The sale would take place at the strike price.

Assignment
If you are selling to open an options contract, and some buyer decides to go ahead with the option and buy or sell the shares, you are said to be "assigned". The process of exercising the option from your point of view is referred to as assignment. This means you are required to sell the shares of stock at the strike price if we are talking about a call option, or you must buy 100 shares of stock at the strike price if instead it is a put option.

Expiration Date for an Option
Every contract has a specified expiration date or exists in perpetuity. For options on stocks, the expiration date is the end date of the options contract. Once it expires, if it hasn't been exercised the contract is no longer in force and it becomes worthless.

In the Money Condition
When an option is in the money that means it is worth exercising, because a profit can be made doing so. If the strike price of a call option is less than the share price on the market, then the call option is "in the money". In the case of a put, the relationship works in the opposite way. That is, if the strike price of the put option is higher than the share price on the market, then the put option would be "in the money".

Out of the Money
An out of the money option is worthless to the buyer, strictly speaking (you can actually earn profits trading out of the money options, however). If the strike price for an option of the call type is higher than the market price, it is out of the money. This is because the buyer of a call option could purchase the shares at a lower price on the open market, so it wouldn't make sense to buy a call option and exercise it with a higher price. For a put option, if the strike price is below the share price it is out of the money.

At the Money
Another condition that can occur is known by the jargon phrase "at the money". If the share price is exactly the same as the strike price of an option, it is "at the money".

Sell to Open
If you are the originator of an options contract, you "sell to open" your position. This means that if it is advantageous to a buyer to exercise an option, you may have to buy or sell shares. There are strategies you can use to avoid having to do so. People that sell to open are looking to use options to earn income. However, if you have an open options contract and a buyer decides to exercise it, you are obligated to meet your end of the deal.

Buy to Open
If you buy to open, you are trading the option, and have no obligations. So, you can sell the option to someone else to close your position, and your obligations cease at that point. If you are looking to acquire stock, you can hold the option to expiration and exercise it. The choice is yours.

Financial Leverage
Options give you large amounts of financial leverage. Although this is the ideal case, the most basic rule of thumb is that a $1 rise in share price will cause the price of a call option to rise by $100. Alternatively, a $1 drop in share price will cause the price of a put option to rise by $100. This is because an options contract represents 100 shares of stock. In fact, it gives you control over those 100 shares of stock for as long as you own the options contract.

We will see that the ideal case isn't always realized, in fact most of the time it isn't. This is because options prices are influenced by many other things, including the days left to expiration, the amount of price fluctuation of the underlying stock (known as volatility), the interest rate, and some other thing such as whether or not it is in the money or out of the money. But the rule of thumb is a pretty good one to keep in mind when you are looking at the possibilities.

The main thing to remember is that you have incredible financial leverage, and the return on investment for options is much higher. If the price of a $200 stock goes up $2, that means if you bought 100 shares for a $20,000 investment, you can make a $200 profit which is just 1%. In contrast, you could potentially double your money buying an options contract instead. That is, you could earn that same $200 profit on a $200 investment buying a single call option. Of course, that is an ideal case, but those kinds of returns are realized on a regular basis by good options traders.

Getting Started with Options

In order to trade options, you will need to have a personal brokerage account. Many readers may not have done that before, and so we are going to briefly explain the process of opening a brokerage account and what your "options" are when doing so in this chapter. We will discuss some of the different brokerages that are available and issues that you need to consider when making your selection.

What is a Broker

A broker is a "middleman". Although there are actual trading floors for options just like there are stock exchanges, you don't actually call in your trading orders directly to the exchange. Instead, a broker does that on your behalf. A broker will provide several things for you, and different brokers provide different levels of support.

At the core, a broker is going to provide you with an account. This is like a bank account of sorts but it's devoted strictly to trading. Options trading is not separate from stock trading, so you will open a brokerage account that will be used to fund trades of both stocks and options, should you decide to invest in both. A brokerage account will be connected to a personal banking account that you provide, so you will connect a bank checking account to the brokerage account. This will be used to transfer funds in and out. So, when you want to buy options, you will need to transfer money into your brokerage account. When you sell options to get money, you may have to wait several days before being able to transfer that money into your bank account. Please check with the broker you select for details.

Like bank accounts, there is a certain amount of government protection for the funds in a brokerage account, should the brokerage go under. This is provided by the Securities Investor Protection Corporation, which insures up to $250,000 cash in your account. Your ownership of actual securities exists outside the brokerage, and if a brokerage were to close your account would be transferred to a new brokerage along with any securities including options that you actively own.

Besides an account, the brokerage will place options trades on your behalf. In order to do this, they will have some kind of interface that allows you to execute your trades. In the old days, this was taken care of with a phone call to the broker or even a personal visit. Today, trades are automatically managed using a software interface. All brokers have a website that can be used to execute trades and move money between the brokerage account and your bank account. Most brokers also have mobile applications.

These are full featured and will allow you to trade stock and options and manage your account on your iPhone, iPad, or Android device. In fact, some brokers are primarily mobile based today, but you can choose the type of interface that you prefer.

Choosing a Broker
There are many different brokers to choose from, and there are many factors that will influence the selection of a broker. The first factor to consider is the interface that the broker uses for trading. You might want to get on YouTube to look for videos posted for different brokerages to see what their trading interface looks like. Some have been designed to be extremely user friendly on mobile, such as Robinhood. However, that may come at a cost.

That cost is on the information side of the system. One of the factors to consider when opening a brokerage account is what tools they provide that can help you manage your trades. In particular, you will be looking for a trading system that will help you get the most information about a trade as possible. Two systems that options traders prefer for this purpose are "Think or Swim" which is run by TD Ameritrade and Tasty Works. These systems were designed by professional options traders to facilitate the trading of options, and so they will contain a lot of the information you will need in order to get a good handle on the potential profitability of a trade, and look at things such as how the expiration date will impact a given trade.

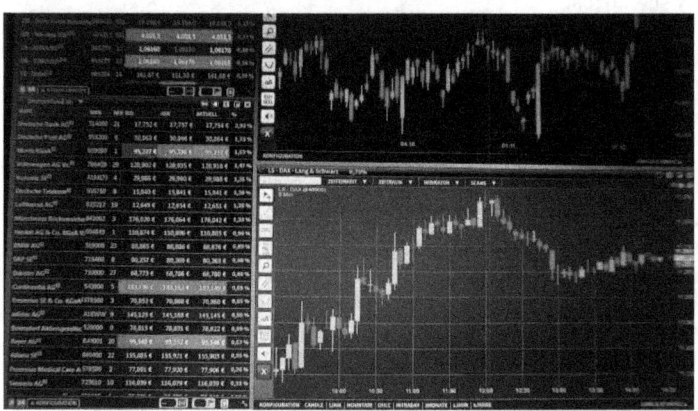

The Think or Swim interface.

Some readers will find the interfaces provided by these platforms to be too complex, and they might prefer the simplicity of Robinhood. Indeed, many beginning traders are gravitating to Robinhood primarily because of its simplicity and ease of use. The Robinhood platform makes it very easy to find options and execute trades, and it also has many setup trades for you to consider and execute with one tap on your smart phone.

Another factor that will be important to some traders is how long a company has been in business and its reputation. If this is important for you, then you can consider a more traditional broker like Charles Schwab or Fidelity. E-Trade, which is not nearly as old as those two companies, has been around for several decades and it has a good reputation among traders as well.

It is important not to sweat your choice of broker too much. If you are attracted to the simple interface of Robinhood, you can actually use other tools in order to do your research. In fact, there are many free tools that can be found on the internet that include using stock charts and calculators that will estimate options values at different dates based on changing stock prices. You can even download fairly accurate calculators for options that are built in Excel spreadsheets. So, while the complete platforms of Think or Swim and Tasty Works suit many traders, you can get a great deal of the information they provide from other sources.

Other things to consider include the amount of support and even advice that is available at the broker. If you are looking for financial advice from a professional, you might be drawn toward a full service broker like Charles Schwab.

Trading Commissions

When I first got in this business, commissions were a big issue to consider. A commission is a fee charged by the broker each time you place a trade. Commissions need to be considered in order to determine whether a trade is profitable or not, and although commissions are not very large in an absolute dollar amount, it can have a major impact in many scenarios.

The good news is that commissions are rapidly disappearing from the industry. In fact, zero commissions options trading was one of the first selling points that was promoted by Robinhood when it came on the scene a few years ago, and this selling point helped to elevate its popularity. This also put competitive pressure on many of the older brokers in the industry.

As a result, many have decided to take the zero commissions route. In fact, Charles Schwab recently introduced zero commissions trading. So, the choices available to traders who are looking for a zero commissions brokerage have massively expanded just in the past year alone. While this used to be a major selling point for Robinhood, that isn't necessarily the case today. But be sure to check with brokers you are interested in to find out the details of their policy with respect to commissions.

Brokers used to rely on commissions as a major source of revenue, so some readers are probably wondering what they are doing now in order to make money. Most brokers offer enhanced services for a fee and this is one way that they make the income they used to make from charging commissions. For example, Robinhood offers a "gold" service with more features for a small monthly fee. Large and established brokers like Schwab may offer professional financial advice to those who are willing to pay for it.

Margin

As you go forward in your trading career, one of the concepts you will need to become familiar with is called margin. In short, margin refers to the ability to borrow from the broker. To do this, you will need to open a "margin account" that will allow you to borrow cash and shares, and enter into certain types of trades that customers without margin accounts cannot do. In order to open a margin account, you must deposit at least $2,500 in cash.

One of the examples of what a margin account allows is that you can do day trading with a margin account (however, day trading requires $25,000 in capital). Margin accounts also allow you to sell "naked" options (we will discuss this in a later chapter) that are not fully backed by hard cash or stocks in your account. For large traders, margin accounts also allow them to borrow shares of stock in order to "short" the stock, that is bet against the stock or bet that the price of the stock is going to drop, and then pocket the profits. That is not something we are going to consider in this book, you will use put options to short stock as an options trader, which is much simpler and something that can be done for a $100 investment rather than having to borrow large numbers of shares of stock, but it illustrates one of the ways that a margin account can be used.

A margin account should be used with care. Like any debt, using it can create risk in the event that you make a bad trade and find it difficult to come up with the cash necessary to cover any losses. However, if you are careful with your use of margin, it can be used to borrow the funds necessary to enter into more complex or larger options trades than you would be able to do using your own money.

Trading Levels

It is also important to familiarize yourself with the different trading levels that exist for options traders. Don't worry if you don't understand everything in this section right away, you can refer back to it as you learn more about trading options. Every broker, however, will have four trading levels for options traders. These are based on your level of experience and your trading goals. When you want to increase your trading level, the broker will require you to go through a quick interview. These interviews are automated so you will answer a few questions on the website or in the brokers mobile app. Something to keep in mind when going through the interview is that you need to make clear that you understand what options are used for and what the regulators expect.

The first thing to note when going through an interview is that you are looking for short-term profits with options. Options are not a long-term investment, although you can trade LEAPS that can last up to two years. But options are not something you invest in for five, ten, or twenty years. The regulators want to make sure you understand this, so you should tell your broker that you are interested in making short-term profits, and that you are not interested in long-term investing. Of course, many readers are going to be interested in doing both, but for the sake of having your trading level increased, you want to put aside your long-term investment goals.

The second thing is to tell the broker that you are interested in "speculation". Speculation basically means you are making a short-term bet on the price of a stock going up or down. Although some types of options trading really aren't speculative, regulators view options as speculative and you should tell them what they want to hear. With that in mind, let's summarize the trading levels that are used by most brokerages.

132

Trading Level One
A level one options trader must back options with cash or assets. A level one options trader is not allowed to buy options in order to trade, you can only sell options. You can sell a covered call, which means you need to own the 100 shares of stock behind the option before selling the call option. Alternatively, you can sell a protected put, which means you must have enough cash in your account in order to buy 100 shares of stock at the strike price, should that become necessary. Anyone who opens a brokerage account is automatically a level one options trader, however you need to have the stock or cash to actually execute a trade. If you already own several hundred shares of stock, level one options trading could be used as a way to generate income from your stock.

Trading Level Two
This level is what most people think about when they are getting into options. Level two trading means that you can buy to open an options contract, and then trade it for a profit. Most readers are going to want to become level two traders. This is usually easy to do. You will just have to open an account and deposit a few hundred dollars, and then go through the broker interview. Level two trading status means that you will be able to buy call and put options.

Trading Level Three
When you start doing options research, you are going to hear about various "strategies" that are used by professional options traders. These include iron condors, strangles, and credit/debit spreads. In order to use these strategies, you will have to be a level three options trader. To do so, your broker will probably require you to have a few months of experience doing level two trading. You will also have to go through another interview.

Trading level Four
Level four options trading is the highest possible level that can be attained by an options trader. A level four options trader is going to be able to engage in any options trade. This includes selling "naked" call and put options. A naked option is one that is not fully backed by cash, but as we will see later you still have to deposit money in your account to help cover naked options. You will also have to open a margin account in order to become a level four options trader. Typically, your broker may also require you to gain some experience first as a level two options trader and then as a level three options trader before they allow you to move up to this level.

133

Day 2: Types of Options

In this chapter we are going to dive into more detail regarding the types of options contracts that are traded. We will explain the important information that lies behind each option and why you want to invest in particular types of options and when to do so.

The Underlying

One of the most significant concepts regarding an option is the underlying. This is the stock that is associated with the option. An option is associated with one and only one stock. So, you can buy an option on IBM, Boeing, or AMD for example.

For the vast majority of options, each option controls 100 shares of stock. So, if you buy an option on Apple, that gives you the right to buy or sell 100 shares of Apple stock.

You can also buy options on many index and exchange traded funds. In fact, some of the most widely traded options are for the S & P 500 or the NASDAQ 100 (SPY and QQQ). Options on index funds give you a way to profit from movements of the overall stock market, and they are highly liquid, which means you can buy and sell them very quickly. This is because of the high volume of trading of options on index funds, which is usually far higher than that seen with individual stocks.

Call Option

A call option gives the buyer the right but not the obligation to buy 100 shares of stock at a fixed price. That fixed price is known as the strike price. A call option comes with an expiration date. You can find options that expire in the current week, over the next few weeks to a month, out to several months to two year from the present date.

Why Invest in Call Options?

You buy a call option when you are bullish on a stock. In other words, you buy a call option when you are expecting the price of the underlying stock to rise. Theoretically, if you are buying a call option, you are hoping to buy shares of stock at the strike price, which you expect to be lower than the market price at some point.

So, let's say that a stock is trading at $99 a share. You could buy a call option with a strike price of $100 a share, if there is a consensus that the stock is going to see a significant rise in prices before the option expires. Say for the sake of example that the option costs you $1. Options prices are quoted on a per share basis, so that means you have to spend $100 to buy the option.

Now say that before the option expires, the share price goes up as expected, say to $103 a share. Now you have two possibilities. When the price of the underlying stock goes up, the value of the option contract goes up as well. Maybe the price of the option has risen to $1.50 per share, say. So, in that case, you can simply sell the option and take the $0.50 per share profit.

You can also choose to exercise the option. This means you can buy the stock at the strike price of $100 a share, even though the market price of the stock has risen to $103 a share. So, your total expense is now $101 a share since you paid $1 to buy the option (assuming zero commissions, which is reasonable these days). So now, you can turn around and sell the stock at $103 a share on the open market, earning yourself a profit of $2 a share. And in some cases, investors may decide to keep the stock that they have now been able to purchase at a discount.

Breakeven Price

An important concept in options trading is the breakeven price. For a call option, the breakeven price is the strike price + the price paid to buy the option, on a per share basis. So, if you are buying an option with a strike price of $212 for $2.50, the breakeven price is simply $212 + $2.50 = $214.50. This means that the share price must rise to at least $214.50 before exercising the option even warrants consideration, otherwise you would be losing money as a buyer. For options sellers, the breakeven price is important to note as well. If you are selling to open call options, you don't have to worry if the market price of the stock stays at or below the breakeven price. In this example, a call options seller would be fine as long as the stock price stayed at or below $214.50.

The Call Seller

An options contract goes on the market when a seller "writes" the contract. For retail traders (individual, small traders) you sell to open from a list of available options. So, you would find a call option with an expiration date and strike price that you like, and then you sell it using your brokerage software. There are three ways that you can sell a call option, the most basic way is to sell a covered call. To do this, you would need 100 shares of the underlying stock. Keep in mind that there is a risk you will lose ownership of the shares, in the event the option is exercised and the shares are "called away" from you. But a carefully selected strike price and expiration date can lower your risk. The goal of selling a covered call option is to generate income from shares of stock that you own. Remember that the breakeven price is going to be something to keep your eye on in this case.

Another way that call options are sold is as a part of one of the options strategies that we will be looking at in later chapters, such as an iron condor or a debit spread. In those types of strategies, there is a single transaction involving multiple options that are bought and sold, and so using a strategy you are never going to be selling a single option.

Finally, you can sell a call option "naked", which means that you don't own the shares of stock. You must be a level four trader in order to sell naked options.

The call seller has a risk of assignment. That means, if the share price rises above the breakeven price, a buyer of an option may choose to exercise the option. As a seller you will be assigned and that means you will be forced to sell 100 shares of stock at the strike price. Many articles about options will assert that most options expire worthless, but the reality is if the option you have sold goes "in the money", there is a real risk that the option will be exercised. In fact, options that expire in the money are often automatically exercised by the broker. Check with your broker to find out their specific policies.

Profits from Call Options

If you are buying call options, then you are hoping to make a profit from either exercising the option or simply selling it at a profit. Most beginning options traders are going to be working with smaller amounts of capital, and so you are probably not going to be interested in exercising the option. Rather, you are going to earn profits from the option itself. As the price of the underlying stock increases, the value of a call option increases as well.

There are several factors working in options pricing, and so you have to take more than just the underlying price of the stock into account. The most important of these is the expiration date. Simply put, the more time there is until an option expires, the more valuable it is. The value in the options price is referred to as time value, and it also makes up a part of "extrinsic" value of the option. With each passing day, the option will lose time value. As we will see in the next chapter, you can actually look up the amount of value that an option is going to lose the following day. At market open, that amount is automatically deducted from the options price. That doesn't mean you can't hold options overnight, because other factors will be operating to push up the price of the option as well, and this may overwhelm the decline in price from the loss of time value. This loss of time value is called "time decay".

136

Options that are out of the money are the most susceptible to time decay, and if they are out of the money as the expiration date approaches, they can be worth hardly anything. When the option actually expires, they are not worth any money at all. That is why we say they "expire worthless".

The most important factor in the price of the option, therefore, is the underlying share price on the open market. For a call option, whenever the share price increases, the value of the option is going to increase. This happens most strongly for in the money options, but all call options will increase in value when there is a movement upward in the share price. So, you can even earn significant profits from out of the money options on a day when there are large upward movements in the price of the stock. These movements don't have to be particularly large, a single dollar rise in share price can mean anywhere from a $50 to $100 increase in the price of an option. So, you could buy an option in the morning and if the share price rises by a dollar during the day, you could sell it for a $50 to $100 profit. The more the share price rises, the more profit is possible. While out of the money options will often yield lower profit amounts for a given share price movement, the profits can still be substantial.

So, for basic options trading, the idea behind buying a call option is simple. You hope to buy low and sell high, earning profits from the upward price movement of the underlying stock. Your goal is to sell the option before expiration and before time decay eats up some or all of the gains (in the case of out of the money options).

As we will see in chapters 7 and 8, call options can also be used as a part of more sophisticated strategies beyond simply anticipating the price of a stock will rise.
Put Option

If you expect the price of a stock to drop, you can profit from this by investing in put options. Put options work in many ways in the same manner as call options. They have an expiration date, they have 100 shares of underlying stock, and their price depends on the price of the underlying stock. Meanwhile, they also suffer from time decay as the expiration date of the option approaches. However, put options actually gain value when the stock price drops, and they lose value when the stock price rises.

This means that put options can be used to "short" the stock. Shorting the stock is just jargon for earning a profit when the stock price declines. Normally, shorting a stock works like this. If you think that a stock is going to drop in value, you borrow shares from your broker – and you immediately sell them on the market at the current stock price. Then, assuming that your bet was the correct one, you buy the shares back when the price drops. Suppose for the sake of example that when you initially borrowed the shares, you sold them at $100 a share. Then the price drops to $80 a share – maybe the company had a bad earnings call, for example. When the price drops, you buy the shares back at $80 a share, and you return them to the broker (remember, you started the process by borrowing shares from the broker). This exercise leaves you with a $20 per share profit.

Of course, most small investors don't have $10,000 or more to chance on schemes like this, but put options enable you to earn profits if the price of a stock declines, using much smaller investments. The idea is basically the same, but when you suspect that the price of a stock is going to drop in the near future, you can buy put options on the stock. A put option has a strike price just like a call option, and when the share price is below the strike price, the put option is in the money. That's because you would be able to buy shares of stock at the market price, and then sell them at the strike price – earning a profit in the process.

Using the same example, we considered before, you could buy a put option with a $100 strike price. Then when the price of the shares dropped to $80, you could buy them on the market, and then sell them to the originator of the put option contract at the strike price - $100 a share. Buying a put option is something that doesn't require a large margin account to do.

When a put option is exercised, that is you sell the stock at the strike price, they say that the stock was "put to" the originator of the option contract. Of course, most options traders are not looking to exercise individual put options. If the stock price were really to drop $20 a share on a stock where you bought put options with a $100 strike price, the value of the put options would go up substantially, because you could exercise them and make solid profits. Since there are other traders who would be interested in selling the stock, you will be able to sell your put option to another trader for a profit. Remember that if you buy to open an options contract, you are not obligated to anything and are free and clear once you sell it to someone else.

Think of put options in the same way as call options, but with the price going up $100 every time the stock drops by $1. Like call options, the pricing of put options is impacted by many factors, and so this is an ideal relationship that we are thinking about here. But it gives you a rule of thumb to understand how put options work (the more in the money they are, the closer they are going to get to the ideal case). Likewise, if the price of the stock rises by $1, the value of a put option would move down by $100. So, with put options, it's an inverse relationship.

Why Buy Put Options
You buy put options when you believe the value of a stock is going to decline. If a company has a bad earnings call, this can be a good time to buy a put option. Typically, the price of the stock will drop a lot, possibly over a day or two, and then stabilize at a new, lower level. Any bad news of any kind provides an opportunity to profit from put options. This is a kind of flexibility that doesn't exist for most stock traders and investors, being able to earn money when stocks are declining. The fact that you can should open your eyes to the potential that options have in expanding your ability to make profits from the stock market. An options trader has the ability to profit under all possible scenarios of stock market movements. As we'll see in chapter 8, a stock trader can even profit from no movement in prices at all!

LEAPS
When you get involved with options trading, you may hear the phrase "LEAPS" mentioned. This is means Long-term Equity Anticipation Securities. This refers to call and put options that have expiration dates ranging from 1-2 years into the future. Since these options have a very long time to expiration, they have a large amount of "time value" and so they are far more expensive. They also lose little value due to time decay. However, they are fairly sensitive to changes in the underlying stock price. LEAPS can represent an opportunity to make profits if you have the capital to invest in them. A call

option on Apple that is slightly in the money expiring in 2 years costs about $4,000. In the next chapter we'll get into the "Greeks" which help us estimate how the option price will change when the price of the underlying stock changes, but for this option it's price will rise $64 for each $1 increase in the price of Apple stock. To get an idea of how time decay impacts LEAPS, a call option with the same strike price that expires a year earlier costs $2,700. It has about the same price sensitivity to the underlying stock.

Other than expiring a long way in the future and having little impact from time decay over the course of a few weeks, LEAPS are no different than any other option. However, there is one particular method experienced traders use that you should be aware of. Some investors use a strategy called the poor man's covered call to leverage LEAPS to sell covered calls. This allows the trader to sell covered calls and earn income with a lower investment, since LEAPS, even though they are pricey compared to short-term options, offer a large discount as compared to actually buying the stock. Consider that Apple is trading at $264 a share, which means 100 shares of Apple necessary to sell a covered call would require an investment of $26,400. That is far more than the $4,000 you'd have to invest in a LEAP that expires in two years.

The details of the poor man's covered call are as follows. First you purchase an in the money LEAP call option. So, in this case we will go with the $260 call at $4,000. Then you sell an out of the money call option that expires in the near term. We can sell a $270 call on Apple that expires in 30 days for $418.

Now we need to calculate the width of the call strike prices. This is:

$270-$260 = $10

Next, calculate the net debit (per share) paid:

$40 - $4.18 = $35.82

The intrinsic value of the LEAP is found by subtracting the strike price from the share price. That is:

$264 - $260 = $4

Over the course of 30 days, if the stock price doesn't change, the LEAP will lose about $1.00 in value, or $100. So, the high strike price option we sold expires worthless, and we keep the $418 we earned. That gives a net profit of $318, and we still have the LEAP. We could sell it, or use it to sell a second call option.

Now let's look at what happens in the case that the stock rises. Suppose that the stock price rises $4 over the 30 days, to $268 a share. In that case, the $270 call we sold against the LEAP still expires worthless, so we earned $418. However, the LEAP actually gains in value in that scenario, probably by about $1.50 per share. We could sell the LEAP at this point for a $147 profit, for a total profit of about $565. Alternatively, you can hold onto the LEAP and then sell another out of the money call against it to earn even more income.

The process can be repeated for a time, but you need to be aware of the time decay that will start to impact the LEAP as the weeks go by.

One risk is that the stock price will rise to the point where the out of the money call goes in the money. Suppose that the share price of Apple rises to $271 by the end of the 30 days. That means we'd have to buy the option back or face assignment. If we buy it back, we will be able to buy it back at a reduced price. The reason is that since the option we sold is so close to expiration, it will lose a lot of value (extrinsic value or time decay) by the time it is 1-2 days from expiration.

However, the LEAP has risen in value by $3.35 at this point. So, we can buy the option we sold back, and we will still be in a position of net profit.

Exercising Options

Options that are in the money will be exercised. This will happen automatically if they expire in the money, with the broker exercising the option. If you are not interested in exercising an option, then sell it before it expires. Keep in mind some brokers like Robinhood have restrictions as to what you can do on the expiration day, so sell your positions the day prior. If you have invested in call options, exercising the option means that you will buy 100 shares of stock at the strike price for each options contract. If you are invested in put options that means you will buy 100 shares of stock and sell them at the strike price for each options contract. While options that expire in the money are often exercised automatically, you have the "option" to exercise them prior to expiration if desired, if the option is "American style". Naturally most options in the United States are American style. If an option is "European style", then they can only be exercised on the expiration date. There are some European style options that are traded in American markets.

Options Chains

Options chains are lists of options that are available on the markets for a given date. In modern trading platforms, this is usually done in a more user friendly manner than what has been used in the past. However, it's a good idea to know how to read them.

When browsing options, the first thing will be to select the expiration date. Some platforms will list call options and put options on the same screen, others will give you a button or tab to switch between viewing call and put options. This is an example ticker from an options chain. So essentially, an options chain is a listing of the tickers assigned to each option for the given expiration date.

GOOG191206C00900000

Let's break this down. The first part of an options ticker is the stock ticker for the stock underlying the option. So, looking at this example, we see that this is an option on Google (Alphabet).

Following this we find the expiration date of the option. It is given in year/month/day format. This means that 191206 tells us that this option expires on December 6, 2019.

Next, the type of option is indicated. A C is used for a call option, and a P is used for a put option.

The last part of the ticker is the strike price of the option. Options prices are given with three decimal places, so the strike price of this option is $900.

As we mentioned earlier, many platforms present options in a more user friendly format. For example, here is how Robinhood lists options:

At the top of the screen, we can select the expiration date. You can also easily move between call and put options, as well as buying and selling, by clicking on the appropriate tab. The current share price is shown right on the screen with the strike prices and required breakeven listed on the left side for each option. The price of the options are shown on the right side. So, at the bottom we see a $1300 call for $12.70. This means that a call option on Google that expires on December 6, 2019 with a strike price of $1,300 would cost us $1,270 (remember to multiply by 100, for 100 shares). Yes, Google options are expensive. That's because the share price is relatively high, over $1k a share.

Factors Determining Options Prices
We have already described some of the factors determining options prices. In the next chapter we will see how those factors are quantified using the Greeks, so that you can make numerical estimates of how options prices are going to change with time. In this section, we will give a complete summary of the factors that impact options prices in a qualitative sense.

The price of the underlying stock is the first factor that impacts options prices. This is a large part of the intrinsic value of the option. That is, it is an "internal" pricing mechanism for the option since it is based on the underlying asset, the 100 shares of stock.

The main thing to know first is that if an option is out of the money, it has no intrinsic value. To illustrate this with a concrete example, let's consider a hypothetical stock with a trading price of $300 a share. We will consider options that expire in 30 days. If there is an option with a strike price of $320 – which is out of the money by $20 – the intrinsic value is zero. If the strike price is $310, half as much out of the money by $10, the intrinsic value is still zero. In fact, if the strike price is at the money at $300, the intrinsic value is still zero.

However, that doesn't mean that the option prices are not impacted by the underlying stock price. Let's look at two examples. First we will consider the $300 strike. With 30 days left to expiration, a call option is priced at $11.35. If the underlying price were to rise to $301, the price of the option would rise to $11.88. That doesn't sound particularly significant, but remember that this is the price per share and there are 100 shares of underlying stock, so this means that the value of the option would rise by $88 with that $1 rise in stock price.

Now let's consider the $310 strike. When the underlying stock is $300 a share, this option costs $7.22. If the share price rises to $301, the $310 strike call option rises in value to $7.61. You could sell the option for a $39 profit – not a bad scenario.

A $1 rise in the stock price of a $300 per share stock is actually quite a small price movement. What if it rises in value by 0.87%, which would be a $2.61 per share increase? In that case, the $310 strike call option would rise in value to $8.26 a share. Now you've made a $104 profit if you sold, with an option that is out of the money by $10 at the start of this scenario.

Now if the strike price is $310 and the underlying stock is $302.61 the value of the option is still entirely "extrinsic" and there is zero intrinsic value. Only in the money options have intrinsic value.

Another factor that impacts the price of an option is volatility. Specifically, implied volatility impacts options prices. Volatility is a measure of how much and how rapidly a stock price changes. If you imagine a stock with wild price swings, that is a volatile stock. If the stock price doesn't change much or increases at a slow, steady rate, that is not a volatile stock.

If a stock is more volatile, that is desirable for options. That's because more volatility means there is a higher probability that an out of the money option is going to go in the money at some point. To see how this works, consider a stock with a share price of $200 a share, with 10 days left to expiration. If we have high implied volatility, say 33%, a $205 call option will have an extrinsic value of $2.36. In contrast, if the implied volatility is 18%, the extrinsic value is only $0.69.

This has an impact on how much the option gains or loses with price movements in the underlying stock as well. If the underlying stock were to increase to $202 per share, if the volatility is 33% the price of the $205 strike call option will go up by $0.74. On the other hand, the 18% volatility case only rises by $0.52. Of course, those are still good gains, we are talking about making a $52 profit from a 1% rise in the share price.

Implied volatility means that we are talking about expected volatility over the lifetime of the option. So, it isn't necessarily going to be the same as the current volatility of the stock. Implied volatility can rise in the future if there is some event coming up that can have a big impact on stock prices. For example, the implied volatility of an index fund can rise in the week before the announcement of GDP growth numbers or unemployment numbers, that can have a large impact on stock prices for the overall market.

Let's look at some real values. A $260 call on Apple that expires in 2 weeks has an implied volatility of 22%. This value isn't impacted much by expiration date. The implied volatility of a LEAP expiring in 2 years has nearly the same implied volatility value.

Different stocks have wildly different implied volatility values. A $330 call on Tesla has an implied volatility of 36% (the current share price is slightly above $335). That means that investors expect the share price of Telsa to fluctuate quite a bit more than the share price of Apple in the coming weeks. Compare these values to Walmart, which only has an implied volatility of 13%. That means a $2 move in the underlying stock price of Tesla will have a much larger impact on the price of the option as compared to the same price move (in percentage terms) on Walmart stock.

Implied volatility impacts in the money options as well. Let's suppose that we have an underlying stock with a $202 share price, and a call option with a $197 strike price. We will stick to the example of 10 days to expiration. If the implied volatility is 33%, the price of the call option would be $7.31.

Now let's keep everything the same and look at changes in the implied volatility. With a 22% implied volatility, the price of a call option would be $6.07. With an implied volatility of 13%, the price of the option would only be $5.27.

So, you see that even with in the money options, different values of implied volatility can have a large impact on options prices. So, one thing to look for when selecting options to trade is you not only want a solid bet that the price is going to move one way or the other, and a good underlying stock price, but you also want more implied volatility as compared to less implied volatility, when all else is equal. Implied volatility impacts the extrinsic value of the option.

You might be trapped into the investor's mindset, and you might be thinking that Walmart and Apple are better "investments" than Tesla. They may be, however as an options trader you are not interested in investment. You are interested in short term price movements – and in this regard Telsa is a better "investment" for an options trader than either Apple or Walmart.

We have already discussed the impact that days to expiration has on options prices. To get a feel for it, let's look at some examples using the tasty trade options calculator. We will look at a call option with a strike price of $215, and an underlying stock price of $220. For the sake of isolating time value, we will leave all other parameters constant, with the exception of days to expiration. We have set implied volatility to 18% for this example.

At 30 days to expiration, the option is worth $745 (or $7.45 per share). At 20 days to expiration, it has dropped to $671. That is a loss of 9.9%. By 15 days, the price has dropped to $6.29. At 10 days, it is $5.83. Notice that the drop from 20 days to 10 days is about 13%, so the option is losing more value as time goes on.

By 5 days left to expiration, the option price has dropped to $533. At 1 day to expiration it's down to $501.

That's how it works for a $5 in the money option. Now let's look at a $5 out of the money option. At 30 days to expiration, a call option with the same parameters except for a strike price of $225, is priced at $253. By 20 days, the price has dropped to $177. Notice that this is about a 30% drop. That quite a bit more substantial than what we saw with the in the money option, which dropped by around 9.9% in the first ten days. The reason for the difference is that an in the money option has intrinsic value, but an out of the money option has no intrinsic value. Intrinsic value stays constant as expiration approaches – assuming no other changes. So, it does give an in the money option some cushion that out of the money options don't have. The intrinsic value for an at the money or out of the money option is always zero. For an in the money option, the intrinsic value is always the share price minus the strike price. For the $215 strike,

143

the intrinsic value would be a constant $5 if the share price didn't change. If the share price rose to $223, the intrinsic value would jump to $8. The difference would mean that at 10 days the option price would be $836, rather than the $583 we calculated above with the unchanging stock price.

By 10 days, the out of the money option has dropped by almost 51% to $87. With the days left to expiration, it's only worth $14, again assuming that nothing else has changed.

The price of the underlying stock, implied volatility, and time to expiration are the main things that impact the price of an option. There are some minor factors that also have some impact, the impact is very small in comparison with these. The process works the same way with put options, except the relationship is reversed for the strike price. Implied volatility and time decay or days to expiration will impact the value of the put option in the same way, but a drop in the price of the underlying stock is favorable for a put option, while an increase in the price of the underlying stock translates into a declining price for a put option.

Day 3: The Greeks

The main factors that impact the price of an option actually go into a mathematical model that governs options pricing. These are labeled as parameters with Greek letters. Although most of us have an aversion to anything "Greek", an options trader should be familiar with the Greeks, which are parameters you can look up at any time when trading options. As we will see, it is not necessary to get into the mathematical details of how they work behind the scenes, you can simply read off the numbers and then interpret them according to simple rules. Let's go through each of them in turn.

Delta: Price of the Underlying Stock

The first "Greek" to consider is delta, a parameter that tells you how the price of an option will move with a price change in the underlying stock. For call options, delta is given as a positive number between 0.0 – 1.0. In the image below, we see the Greeks for a Facebook call option:

What this tells you is that the price of the option will move up or down by 58.97% of the price change of the underlying stock. Or more simply, if the price of the stock were to rise by $1, the price of the option (for 100 shares) would rise by $58.97. Likewise, if the price of the stock dropped by 40 cents, the price of the option would drop by $23.59, which is 58.97% of $40.

Delta is influenced by all the factors that influence options pricing. The more in the money an option is, the larger delta is going to be. For example, if an underlying stock has a share price of $223, and the strike price of a call option is $222 with five days left to expiration, delta is 0.57, meaning that the price of the option will rise and fall by $57 for every $1 rise or fall in the underlying stock price. On the other hand, if the strike price is $210, with five days left to expiration delta is 0.99, and so the option price will rise or fall by $99 for every $1 rise or fall in the underlying stock price.

The longer there is to expiration, the lower delta is. That is because the underlying stock price is less influential when there is a long time to expiration – because an option has more of its price tied up in extrinsic value (specifically in time value). Using the above example, a $210 strike price and a $223 share price, with 30 days to expiration delta is 0.83, and so rather than moving by $99 with a $1 change in underlying stock price, the option price would only move by $83, meaning that the stock price is about 19% less influential when there is more time for this particular option to the expiration date. In all cases the price of the underlying stock is going to be less influential when there is more time to expiration, but it will not be 19%, it will be some other value.

Consider an out of the money option. So, we have a $223 share price and say a $225 strike price. Delta in this case is 0.46. While this is quite a bit smaller than for an in the money option, you can see it is still quite substantial. If you bought the option in the morning and the share price went up by $1, the price of the option would jump from $497 to $543 (or a little more). So, you can still experience significant profits for out of the money options. Check delta to get an estimate.

Of course, changes in the stock price are going to change delta. But let's keep the $223 stock price and look at how delta changes with time for this out of the money option. What we find is delta changes, but not by drastic amounts. With 15 days left to expiration, in this case delta has dropped to 0.43. Of course, the price of the option has dropped significantly, to $325. That happened because of the loss of time value. So, delta remaining somewhat constant isn't an argument in favor of holding onto out of the money options over a long time period if there isn't a chance of them going in the money.

With everything else being held constant, as the expiration date approaches delta loses significant value. With just three days to expiration, an out of the money option (in this case to remind we are out of the money by $2) has a delta of 0.34.

The more out of the money you are, the smaller delta is going to be. If we are $5 out of the money, with 3 days left to expiration delta would be 0.14, which is significantly smaller. Again, buying out of the money options isn't necessarily the best idea, but it can work for short term trades. Suppose that you bought 10 of these options and the price of the stock went up by $1 on that day, that would mean that you would have the potential to sell the options for a $140 profit (that could raise some day trading issues, however, since options are subject to day trading rules).

For put options, the concept is the same, but delta is expressed as a negative number, because of the inverse relationship between the option price and the share price of the underlying stock.

For a specific example, consider a put option with a strike price of $225 and an underlying stock price of $221. Since the strike price is higher than the underlying share price, and we are talking about a put option, this means that we are talking about an in the money option. The price of the put option with 10 days to expiration is $574, and delta is -0.67. That tells us that if the stock rises in price by $1, the price of the option is going to drop by about $67. On the other hand, if the price of the underlying stock drops by $1, that makes the put option more valuable, and the price of the put option would increase by about $67.

Otherwise, the relationships work the same way. As time passes for an out of the money put option, which means that the strike price is below the current share price, the magnitude of delta gets smaller. In contrast, if the put option is in the money, which means the strike price is higher than the share price, the closer it gets to expiration the higher delta is going to be. This happens for the same reason it does with call options, that is as a put option that is in the money approaches expiration, the extrinsic value of the option is dropping to near nothing while the intrinsic value varies with the difference between the strike price of the option and the share price of the underlying shares of stock.

Delta is one of the most important of the Greeks that options traders keep an eye on. The next one is theta, which we take up in the next section.
Theta
The next Greek that we will consider is theta. This Greek is a quantifiable measure of time decay. It will give you an idea of how much your option will decline in value the

following market open. Each day when markets open, options held overnight lose value automatically due to time decay. Since this represents a decline in value, theta is listed as a negative number. For example, if we have an option with a strike price of $225 and the underlying share price is $221 with ten days to expiration, theta is -0.15 for both the call and the put option, which are priced at $176 and $574, respectively. The following day at market open, the prices of the call and put options will immediately drop to $161 and $559.

Theta is going to change with time, but it changes slowly. The following day theta increases a bit, moving to -0.158 for the call option and -0.157. This will help you understand how much value your option is going to lose with each passing day.

Of course, like anything else, the example we've used to illustrate this holds everything else constant, so that we can focus on theta and how it describes what happens to options prices. At market open, however, prices of shares are going to be very actively moving. Suppose that the share price increases to $222.50. When the underlying share price changes, theta will change as well. And it turns out that the underlying share price actually has more influence on theta than the passage of a single day of time. So, while the passage of time increased theta a little bit, raising the share price by $1.50 increases theta to about -0.17 for both the call and the put. If the share price rose even more, to say $225 a share, theta for the call would increase to -0.181, while theta for the put would rise to -0.179. Of course, this would have more impact on the price of the options than on theta, but it is important to be aware of what happens to theta as share prices move.

So, let's say that you had the call with the $225 strike price, and the share price was at the money at $225 at market close. At this point, the call is $325. The next day, the simple passage of time would drop that call to $306 at market open, and theta would increase to -0.192.

However, if the stock rally continued, and say the share price of the stock rose by an additional $2, by the end of the day the call option would be $418. That might be a good time to sell your option for a profit since it gained a substantial amount of value. That also causes theta to drop a little bit to -0.186.

Sometimes stocks can move by huge amounts based on news, and certainly after earnings calls. When you are approaching an earnings call, implied volatility can also rise to very high levels. Let's suppose that implied volatility went to 40%. That would spike the price of the option to $641, but keep in mind that theta also increases, this time to -0.331. The following morning, that means that the option would drop in value to $606. Theta would increase even further, to -0.353.

Now suppose that night they have an earnings call, and it beats expectations. We are going to talk about the importance of earnings calls more in a later chapter when we discuss strangles and straddles, but for now just note that earnings calls can result in very large moves in stock prices. A positive earnings call for a $227 stock might cause it to jump $20 or more in price, during off-hours trading.

Let's move to day 6, and increase the share price to $247. That will bump up the price of the option to $2,218. But the implied volatility will drop, since the earnings call has happened and the stock has made the big move everyone was waiting for. That won't impact the price of the option much, it will stay around $2,200. Theta, however, will drop down quite a bit, because now the call option is well within the money with six days left to expiration (in fact, delta gets very close to 1.00 in this scenario).

So, to summarize, theta represents the amount of value that the option is going to lose overnight from time decay. It is expressed as a price, so if you see a theta of -0.12, that means that the option is going to decline in value by 100 x 0.12 = $12.

In addition to being impacted by the passage of time, changes in share price throughout the day can have a large impact on the value of theta. The direction isn't as important as it is how far the share price is from the strike price. The further the share price is from the strike price; the smaller theta is going to be.
The maximum value of theta is going to occur when the option is at the money – when the share price is equal to the strike price. No matter which direction the share price moves off the strike price, the more it moves the smaller theta is going to be, both for the call and the put option with the same strike price.

Finally, the higher the implied volatility, the higher theta goes.
Gamma
Gamma is a lesser known Greek. It's actually secondary, telling us how rapidly delta will change. The way it works is quite simple. If gamma is 0.03, say, and delta was 0.54 for a call option, and the share price went up by $1, delta would change to 0.57. Alternatively, if the share price dropped by $1, if gamma were 0.03 and delta was 0.54, it would drop delta to 0.51.

So, in other words, gamma tells us how much delta will change for every $1 change in share price. Gamma is the same value for call and put options with the same strike price and expiration date, but it works inversely. That is, if delta for a put option was -0.46, with gamma equal to 0.03, then a $1 rise in share price would make delta drop to -0.43, but a drop in share price by $1 would make delta increase negatively to -0.49.

If implied volatility goes down, gamma increases in value. If implied volatility increases, gamma decreases in value. If an option is a long way from expiration, gamma tends to be small. However, as the option nears expiration date, gamma will increase. As an example of this, consider a stock trading at $302 a share. Suppose that we have a strike price of $300. Remember – gamma is the same for both call and put options at the same strike price.

At 22 days to expiration, gamma will be 0.03. At 10 days to expiration, gamma has increased a little bit, to 0.04. At 2 days to expiration, gamma has risen to 0.09 – more than double what it was at 10 days to expiration. This reflects the fact that an option closer to expiration is going to be impacted more by price changes in the underlying stock, because more of the options value comes from intrinsic, rather than extrinsic value (and time value).

148

Since gamma is the same value for call and put options, whether the option is in or out of the money isn't what's important in determining its value. It's the absolute distance of the strike price from the share price that is important. Gamma is at the highest value when the strike price is equal to the share price, that is if the option is at the money.

It's interesting to look at the value of gamma for LEAPS. If an option is a very long way from expiration, 300 days or more, gamma assumes pretty small values. It might be at 0.01 or less.

Finally, let's look at implied volatility. If implied volatility is higher, gamma will be lower. If implied volatility is small, then gamma will be higher. The factor in the difference between different implied volatilities will be about the same as the difference in scale of gamma values. That is, if the implied volatility is 1/10th as small, gamma will be 10 times as large, and vice versa.

Vega

As we discussed in the last chapter, the implied volatility of an option can have a pretty significant impact on options prices. Higher implied volatility will increase options prices, and options traders often prefer higher levels of implied volatility. Since this is one of the crucial factors that determines the price of an option, there is a Greek for that – and it is called vega. Keep in mind that vega has the same value for call and put options that have the same strike price and expiration date.

Vega is a decimal value that will tell you how sensitive the options price is to a 1% change in the implied volatility. To see how it works, like anything else with options it is helpful to look at concrete examples.

Let's return to our example of a stock trading at $302 a share. Like some of the other parameters we've looked at, vega is at the highest value when the strike price is equal to the share price, that is for an at the money option. The further the strike price is away from the share price, the smaller vega will be. The impact is fairly large. Let's illustrate this with an implied volatility of 5% (chosen small so we can study the difference of a large implied volatility in a minute).

So, if the strike price is $302 for an at the money situation, vega will be 0.141. A call and a put will be priced at $71 and $70 in this situation if there are five days to expiration. If the implied volatility went up a single percentage point to 6%, the call and the put would both increase in value to $85 and $84 respectively. So, you can see that they increased in value roughly by $14. So, we can take the value of vega and multiply by 100 to see how many dollars the value of an option would increase (or decrease) by for every 1 percentage point change in implied volatility.

Increasing the volatility while holding everything else the same doesn't have very much impact. In fact, vega doesn't change at all under that scenario. So, with a strike price of $302 and 5 days to expiration, vega is the same if the implied volatility is 5%, and at 18%. In fact, the implied volatility could be any value between 1-100% and vega would remain 0.141. It starts decreasing if implied volatility goes over 100%, which is possible but extremely rare.

What about the expiration date? The further you are from the expiration date, the higher vega is. At one year from expiration, vega would be 1.193. So that would mean a 1% change in implied volatility could mean a $119.30 increase in the price of an option, all other things being equal.

This should make the light bulbs go off in your head. In situations where you expect implied volatility to increase – such as an approaching earnings call – you can make big profits on options that are far from the expiration date. This works especially well with LEAPS, but also works when you are a month to six weeks or so to expiration. At 30 days to expiration, vega is 0.345, meaning that a 1% rise in implied volatility will lead to a $34.50 increase in the price of the option. Implied volatility can go up by huge margins as earnings calls approach, so this can give you a good opportunity to earn profits. You can buy call and/or put options on a stock a month prior to an earnings call, and watch as implied volatility goes up and adds to your options prices, generating profits.

We will stick to the $302 strike. At 30 days to expiration with an implied volatility of 19%, a call option is priced at $660, with vega equal to 0.345. Suppose that by 15 days to expiration, implied volatility is 70% (yes, you sometimes see this). In this case, the price of the option has increased to $1,710 – and you could sell at this point making a nice profit of more than $1,000.

Implied volatility is going to increase if investors think that there are going to be big moves in the stock price, no matter what happens. So, it won't matter to you if a good or bad earnings call is expected, or whether that actually happens. The anticipation of the upcoming earnings call and large price movements in the stock can be enough to send options prices soaring, because implied volatility will be rising by large amounts. Vega will decrease as you get closer to expiration, but often that won't be a factor, because in the meantime it keeps adding more and more value, far outstripping the value lost to time decay.

Rho

The final Greek that we need to take note of is Rho, but in today's environment it's not that significant as compared to the others. Rho is a measure of the sensitivity of options prices to changes in interest rates. Specifically, it is based on a somewhat hypothetical "risk free" interest rate that is generally taken to be the interest rate on a ten year U.S. Treasury. If the interest rate goes up by a large amount, call options will rise in value and put options will decrease in value. If interest rates drop, put options will increase in value and call options will decrease in value. Rho is generally pretty small; a typical value might be around 0.06 for a call option and -0.06 for a put option. The value of Rho tells you how much a one percentage point change in the risk free interest rate is going to impact the price of the option. Generally speaking, it's not very important to worry about. In the late 1970s, interest rates rose rapidly to very high values, so in that kind of environment (or one in which interest rates were rapidly decreasing) it might be significant. But in today's environment, it is not something that you should worry about or base your trading and investment decisions on.

Minor Greeks?

That is our summary of the major Greeks. There are even more Greeks, that are called the minor Greeks. These go by color, epsilon, lambda, speed, ultima, vera, vomma, and zomma. These are more obscure and can be used by large professional traders that have sophisticated computer models, but for the vast majority of traders these extra Greeks are not worth worrying about (even rho is not really worth worrying about, and gamma is even a bit questionable to devote attention to). For most traders, delta, theta, and vega give you all the information that you need to know in order to have a solid foundation upon which to manage your trades.

Day 4: Designing a Trading Plan

Far too many beginners set themselves up for trouble when they begin trading options by not having a plan. If you want to earn consistent profits when trading options, it is important to have a solid trading plan, and to be disciplined when carrying out your trades. These days, trading options is pretty easy. In some ways, that is a great thing. However, it can also lead people into trouble. If you just trade options on a whim, that can end up leading to quick losses.

Options prices can move fast. A simple moment of thought illustrates what can happen. Since the price of an option could move by $50, $75, or even $90 for a mere $1 rise or decline in the price of a share of stock, it's very easy for options prices to move very quickly. These rapid and dramatic price movements can create a lot of problems for new traders, and if you are only buying and selling individual call and put options, you are going to be very susceptible to these issues. If you were to buy five call options, and the stock price dropped by $1 with a delta of 0.75 over the course of ten minutes, you would lose $375.

And if you get in a situation like that, without a trading plan you won't be sure what to do. Often, stock prices can quickly reverse, and a $1 rise or fall of a stock price isn't all that significant for many of the most popular stocks, that have share prices that range from $100 to $2,000 per share. So, a $1 move in share price is not something necessarily unprecedented.

So, one of the problems with a big drop in price is that panic may ensue, and a novice trader will sell out to cut their losses. This can turn out to be a bad decision in many cases, and so selling options when there is a loss like that is not necessarily something that is the right decision. In this book we will introduce the topic of technical analysis to help you learn ways to determine when to get in and out of trades, but the point here is that you need to have a plan in place rather than trading on emotional impulse.

This can work the other way as well. If the price of a share rises by $1, you could end up with significant gains (for the sake of example and simplicity, we are assuming that you are trading call options). One of the problems that happens with novice traders, is they get overwhelmed with irrational exuberance when share prices are rising. If the share price rises by $1, and you have five call options that rise in value by $345, it's easy to start having visions of making $1,000 in an afternoon. But of course, what often happens is a $1 rise in share price can suddenly turn into a $2 loss, and it can do that in a matter of minutes.

Trading Psychology
To avoid making these kinds of mistakes, it is important to adopt a trading psychology. In short, this means having a strict plan that you follow at all times. In a sense, you need to be detached from your trading on an emotional level, as if you were not the one risking the money. Of course, this is not something that is always easy to do. If you are losing your own hard earned money, it can be difficult to detach yourself emotionally from what's going on.

The way to do this is to setup rules ahead of time and follow them. As a part of your trading psychology, becoming organized and disciplined is going to be something that you need to master. If you are not the kind of person who is organized and prone to detailed planning, then you will need to adjust your approach to things.

An important part of the trading psychology is not giving into emotion. As we mentioned in the introduction, you can fly into a panic when you get large losses, and you can also become excessively elated when you get gains. When you let emotion guide your trading decisions, you are going to find that you make a lot of mistakes. Sometimes, luck will be involved and so traders who are prone to making emotional decisions and not carefully planning out their trades are still going to have some impressive wins. This helps to keep them addicted and bring them back to make many trades, and if they get a big winning trade it will encourage them to keep following the same impulsive process hoping to hit another big win.

The best trading psychology is one that begins with a long-term plan. You should sit down and figure out what your long-term goals are over different time frames. First off, you need to be thinking in terms of reasonable gains. You are not likely to build success by hoping to make a million dollars right away. Instead, think in terms of making $100 a week, or $200 a week. Then map out a strategy that is going to help you actually realize your goals. Then once you have reached the goal, you can set a new goal to increase your income.

Trading options is not something that you can do if you have a "set it and forget it" attitude. As an options trader, although you don't necessarily have to be glued to your computer all day long, you need to be carefully tracking the movements in the share price of any underlying stock for your options. You don't want to impulsively buy an option (or ten options) and then go off and forget about them. You should be checking regularly to see how your options are doing, and possibly using electronic tools to setup alerts and so forth.

Trading Journal
It is my belief that every options trader should keep a written record of their activities in a trading journal. Start the journal by mapping out your goals for the next 3 months. Include the amount of money you want to earn and develop a plan to reach your goal. Then include a record of all your trades in the journal. Include the date you enter the trade, how many options you bought or sold, and the amount of capital involved. Then when you close out your trade update your entries with the final results. It is important to keep a record and be honest with yourself. One of the mistakes that impulsive and emotional traders make is they don't keep a record of their actual trades. That makes it easy to fool yourself into thinking that you are breaking even or even making a profit, when in fact you are losing money.

You should also keep a record of your results, including profits and losses for each trade and any other expenses. This can be kept in written form or by using a spreadsheet. This will help you determine whether or not you have a winning trading program and know your actual net gain or loss. It is important to be realistic about where you are and how well you are doing in reaching your goals, and keeping a detailed record rather than winging it is one way to do that.

If you find that you are constantly having losing trades, then you shouldn't keep doing what you've been doing. Obviously in the beginning you can expect to possibly lose money on several of your first trades, and you might lose money on multiple trades in a row. That is fine in the first few weeks of trading, but if you find after a month you are continually losing money on your trades, you will need to take a step back and do some analysis to find out the reasons why you keep losing on trades. Write down everything about the trade, including how long you stayed in the trade, what made you pick the trade, how much was invested, and so on. Are you holding on too long? Getting out too prematurely? Investing in options right before earnings calls and getting hammered by bad decisions? Getting in on a rising stock price too late, only to find that you mistimed it and the stock price started dropping soon after you entered into your positions?

When you do your analysis and come up with some adjustments to your trading approach, then you can resume trading with an updated training plan. Keep in mind that this is a work in progress, and you don't have to expect success immediately.

Be Realistic: It is not all wins

Many traders think they are not doing well if they don't win on every trade. The reality is that even the best options traders are going to experience losses. The goal is to win more often than you lose so that you have net profits. Over time as you gain experience, you can expect to improve your performance.

Value Education

The fact that you're reading this book is a great sign! Those who are willing to study and learn are definitely going to be more successful than those who simply start trading on impulse. But don't let this book be the end of your education, it should only be the beginning. There are many resources available for those who want to trade options, and you should continually take advantage of them. The more that you can learn about options trading, the more likely it is that you are going to be successful. You should watch as many videos as you can find, learn all the different ways and strategies that can be used when trading options, and read as many books and educational materials as possible.

You should look for official information about options that can help you learn the ropes from experienced traders. Many organizations that are associated with options trading have educational materials available. I also strongly recommend that you follow tasty trade. This is a group associated with the options trading platform Tasty Works, but you don't have to have an account with Tasty Works to use the educational platform. They have a large number of educational videos which are free to view on their website and on YouTube. They also have talk shows where they discuss different trading results, approaches to trading, and interviews with people who became successful options traders. Since it's free and put together by people who have been professional options traders for many decades in some cases, this is one of the best resources that you can use to educate yourself about trading options.

Use Buying and Selling Calls as a Learning Opportunity

Many novice traders have visions of making millions of dollars buying and selling individual call options. It is possible to make money trading individual call and put options, however very few professional traders make a career doing so. The fact is that straight trading of individual options is not likely to bring consistent and long-term success. It is just too difficult to consistently predict which way a stock price is going to move over short time periods.

That said, everyone has to start as a level 2 trader, and you can look at the period of time that you spend trading call and put options as a chance to gain some experience. At first, start with single options contracts until you get used to the mentality and experience of options trading.

As you train yourself, although many will be tempted to stick with call options because they are the way people think (you make money when the stock rises in price), you should also look for opportunities to make money from put options, and trade them. This will help your skills as an options trader broaden and improve, and you will start learning how to recognize trends in the markets that move in both directions.

Adopt a Trading Type

We haven't gotten into all the trading strategies yet. But by the time you finish this book, you will understand all the main ways that you can trade options and the main strategies that are used by professional options traders. As you are learning, you can try your hand at all of them and find out which ones you enjoy the most and which ones you are best at trading.

However, you should winnow out your trading methods. The best professional traders are those that focus on using only one or two trading strategies. Options traders that become sellers of options premium typically only sell options premium. Of course, some people are able to multi-task more than others, and so they may have a more diversified strategy. The traders on Tasty Trade are often using many different strategies. That said, when you are new options trader, it is good to find one or two strategies and then master them. If you are able to work up a solid profit over the course of a year, then at that time you might want to expand your trading repertoire.

As another example, many traders like using iron condors to generate income. A large number of traders only trade iron condors. They have become expert at using this one technique, and so they spend their time looking for opportunities to apply the strategy, and earning regular income.

Equipment and Location

Most options traders don't need a large amount of equipment. If you start saying the word "trader", you are probably approaching this issue thinking of day traders with banks of computer screens displaying lots of charts and tables. This is not necessary for the vast majority of options traders. You certainly should have a good desktop computer that you have access to, and optionally you should also have a smart phone or tablet you have access to as well. If you are using a trading platform that does not have a lot of analysis tools and you have to use a second website for that purpose, you might want to have a second desktop computer or use a second device like an iPad to be following stock charts and so forth. Most traders can get by with a good desktop computer, iPad, and smart phone. And of course, you will need a good internet and Wi-Fi connection. The last thing you want to do is get in a situation where you are needing to get out of a trade and your internet connection goes down. This is one reason why having a smart phone so that you can still access the trading platform when your internet is down is a good idea, rather than relying exclusively on a desktop computer.

You can trade at home and then use a smart phone to keep tabs of your trading when not at home. It is recommended that you set aside a space for your trading activities. This is a part of viewing your options trading as a business. If you were to start an at home business, you would probably set aside some home office space for it. Do the same when it comes to your options trading.

Trading as a Business

Options trading is flexible. You don't have to dive into options trading full time if you don't want to. You can do it very part-time, and set a goal of only making a few hundred dollars a month, or you can go full-fledged into options trading and try and build a million dollar a year business.

Trading as a business can, but doesn't necessarily have to, mean setting up an actual business for your trading activities. Depending on the laws of your location, you can setup a corporate entity and use that for your trading activities. Approaching it in that way will require satisfying all of the legal requirements, including tax forms, and setting up separate bank accounts. This is not an accounting book or one that provides legal advice, so please check with an accountant for details.

Of course, it is not necessary to setup a business for options trading. You can certainly do it and just treat it as individual income. Keep in mind that options trading – for the most part – is going to involve short term capital gains. In the United States short term capital gains are treated as regular income for tax purposes. If you do invest in LEAPs and hold some assets for a year or longer, you may be able to treat your gains as long-term capital gains, and get preferential tax treatment.

You are unlikely to run into any legal trouble with the one exception being opening a margin account. If you open a margin account and are unable to meet your debt obligations, then you could get into some trouble. That might be something to consider when thinking about whether or not you start your trading activities as an official business to separate it from your personal activities. But for most people it shouldn't be necessary to go through all the trouble of setting up a business when it comes to options trading.

Risk Management

One of the most important things to get a handle on when you begin trading options is a plan for risk management. On the losing side, this means having a "stop loss". That is a value you use to determine when to exit a trade. So, if the options price were to drop say $50, you can setup your trading platform to automatically sell any options that fit this description. Alternatively, you can also setup trades to automatically sell when you reach a certain level of profit. This is called a "take profit". Check to see if your trading platform allows you to enter automatic stop loss and take profit orders.

If you can, this will greatly simplify your trading activities, and keep you from making impulsive and emotional mistakes. Instead, you will be able to cap your losses on any given trade, and ensure that if stock prices are rising, you get out with profits without waiting too long because you get excited and greedy. Remember, that can lead to losses. It is better to put caps, which of course means that you are going to miss out on some gains from time to time. But more often than not, it means that you are going to avoid making large mistakes. It is better to consistently make $50 profits, rather than holding on too long all the time hoping to score big and ending up with small profits or even losses.

If your system does not allow you to enter automatic stop loss and take profit orders, you are going to have to develop some personal discipline and manage those manually. That means that you would have to pay attention to your gains and losses, and be ready to exit trades when the rule you have decided upon is realized.

There are no hard rules to follow, you will have to pick something that works for you. But in my opinion, on a per option basis, a maximum loss of $25 is reasonable. So, if you enter into a trade and you are losing $25 per options contract, you should go ahead and sell your options. This is a matter of cutting losses without letting them get out of control while you hope that things get better. Also, it will keep you from panicking too easily, by setting a fairly significant loss level, you will keep yourself from jumping out too early when the stock is going to reverse and make profits for your options.

On the other side, for take profit, take a 2-to-1 to 4-to-1 ratio. So, if you are going to have a $25 stop loss limit, then set your take profit to $50, or possibly $100, per options contract or trade.

These rules are not going to guarantee profits. Sometimes they are going to work to provide winning trades, and sometimes this is not going to appear to help you. What you are looking for is a systematic approach that will help you to earn profits on average. The specific values you pick are less important than simply having some kind of risk management system. Of course, you don't want to be too conservative, because then you will be missing out on a lot of profits and getting out of many trades too early.

And don't stop here. Remember that we said you should be aiming to continually educate yourself as an options trader. So, get online and find out what other options traders are doing, and settle on the type of risk management system that fits you the best. Remember that different traders are going to have different levels of risk tolerance.

Day 5: Technical Analysis

Professional traders often use a set of tools known as technical analysis in order to help them make better trades. Specifically, technical analysis can help you detect developing trend reversals in stock charts, and this information can help you get into and out of your trades at the best possible time. Technical analysis is a favorite tool of day and swing traders, and some options traders use it, but not all options traders do. Nonetheless, you should have some familiarity with it to determine if it is something you feel could help your trading.

Technical analysis involves a wide range of tools. These include looking at moving averages and specialized types of charts known as candlestick charts. Some traders also look for stock chart patterns that can signify a trend reversal, or change in price momentum.

It's important not to get too enamored with technical analysis. That is, you don't want to get into a mindset where you view technical analysis as "fact", because the cold truth about technical analysis is that it is a tool and nothing more. It is too easy to put far too much faith into technical analysis that really isn't deserved. Nonetheless, technical analysis is definitely a useful tool, and you can pick and choose specific tools of the trade that you feel will help you make more educated trading decisions. In this chapter I will briefly review the trading tools that I personally believe are the best ones to use when trying to find the best times to get in and out of options trades.

Studying Trends with Moving Averages
The most important thing on a stock chart that a trader is going to look for on a stock chart is a trend reversal. If you are looking to profit from call options, then what you are going to look for is a relatively low stock price, or a stock price that is in decline, and then wait for it to show signs of a reversal. In other words, this is going to help you buy low, and sell high. So, the technique once you have entered a position is to study the charts looking for the coming reversal once the price has peaked, and so you can exit your position.

Moving averages are the easiest tools to use for this purpose. What a moving average does is it takes several time periods of stock data, and at each point, it calculates the average, out to a fixed number of points. The definition of a "point" is up to the individual trader, it could be an hour, a four-hour period, a day, or a week. It could even be five-minute intervals. If you are planning on trading an option over a 30 day period, then you will probably be looking at using days for your time frame. In that case, a 9-period moving average would calculate the average of the closing price at each day, using the past nine days to do the calculation.

In order to spot trend reversals, traders rely on using moving averages with different periods (but they will use the same definition of period, be it day, week, or five minutes). So, you could use a 9-period moving average, and a 20-period moving average. Alternatively, you might use a 50-period moving average, and a 200-period moving average.

Obviously a longer-period moving average is going to give you more information on the historical pricing level of the stock in question. Different types of moving averages are going to treat this in different ways. A simple moving average will do a standard mathematical average of all data points. So, if we had a 9-period simple moving average for closing prices of Apple, on a particular day it might calculate:

$$SMA = (212.41 + 213.11 + 212.50 + 214.29 + 215.72 + 216.01 + 217.22 + 217.50 + 216.95)/9$$

Many traders are completely content to use the simple moving average, but if you look at how it's calculated, you should note that all prices are treated the same. This is objectionable, because if you are looking to make a trade, recent prices are going to be more important to you than historical, older prices. We certainly want information from the historical pricing level of the stock, but it is more recent prices that are going to have the most impact on our trading decisions. For this reason, many traders use weighted moving averages, that give more weight to recent closing prices and less weight to closing prices in the past. There are two very popular weighted moving averages that are used, the Hull moving average, and the more popular exponential moving average.

In order to detect a trend reversal, you will use two moving averages on your stock chart of the same type, but with different period lengths. So, you can use a nine day period exponential moving average with a 20-day period exponential moving average. No matter what type you choose and what periods you use, there are only two rules you need to worry about.

The first rule is known as a golden cross. This happens when the short-period moving average curve crosses above the long-period moving average curve. This tells you that the stock is likely to be entering an upward trend. In the example below, a 50-day simple moving average and a 200-day simple moving average are used. Notice that after the golden cross (the 50-day moving average crossing above the 200-day moving average), the stock enters into a relatively long-term upward trend.

The beauty of this tool is that it is very simple to use – it is also something that a beginning trader can understand quite easily.

160

Of course, stocks are not always going up, otherwise everyone would be rich. So, we have to know how to spot the development of a downward trend in prices as well. This is indicated by a so-called death cross. In a death cross, the short-period moving average curve crosses below the long-period moving average curve.

This is clearly illustrated in the chart below, which shows a death cross for Facebook, and the drop in stock prices that followed:

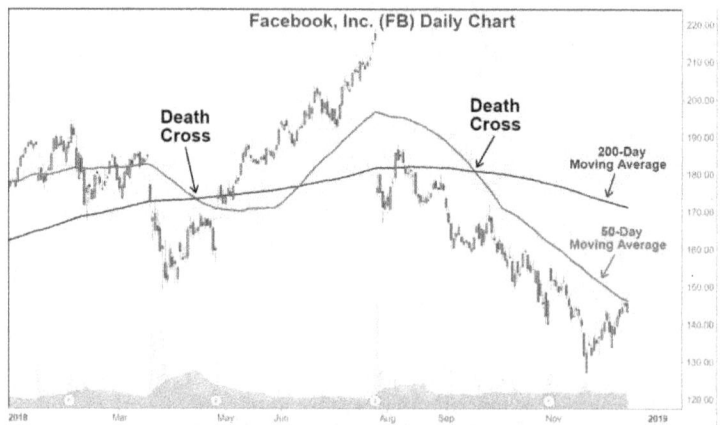

The question now is how to use crosses of moving average curves with options trading. You should see from the examples that it's actually quite simple. When you are looking to get into a trade, you should add the appropriate moving averages to your charts, and then use a golden cross or a death cross as a signal to enter or exit trades.

For call options, you want to enter a trade when there is a golden cross. Then, when the chart shows a death cross, exit your positions. It's that simple.

For put options, you will do the opposite. That is, you will wait to enter your trade until you see a death cross. For options traders, since you can profit either way, a "death" cross is also a signal for profits, but with using put options. Then you hold your position until you've either reached a level of profit you are comfortable with or you see a golden cross, indicating a coming trend reversal.

Remember that with options, the expiration date and time decay are always lurking in the background, so you don't necessarily want to wait for another crossing to occur before exiting your positions. Each case will have to be evaluated individually.

Momentum

One of the most important concepts that stock traders look for is momentum. Price momentum occurs when a large number of traders are either buying or selling a stock, pushing prices strongly in one direction or another. The tool that you can use to study the momentum of a stock price is called the Relative Strength Indicator. You can add this to your stock charts to help you study the best times to get into and out of positions to maximize possible profits.

The relative strength indicator will be displayed below your stock chart. It is a curve that can go between 0 to 100. Typically, the values 0-30 and 70-100 are what traders are looking for on the chart. When the curve goes into the range of 0-30, this means that a stock is "oversold". That is, traders have sold off too many shares, pushing prices down to a level that makes it likely that new traders are going to now find the stock an attractive buy, and so they are likely to start loading up on the stock, and pushing prices upward again. The lower the RSI gets, the stronger this signal is.

On the other hand, if the RSI goes into the range of 70 and above, this indicates overbought conditions. In this case, frantic purchasing of the shares has pushed prices up too high, and traders are likely to start getting out of the stock, because they want to get out before the price drops when there is a large selloff.

The RSI should not be taken in isolation. A good way to use it is to use it in conjunction with the moving averages. So, if you see oversold conditions with the RSI, together with a golden cross, that indicates that stock prices are likely to start moving upwards. On the other hand, if the RSI indicates overbought conditions, and you also see a death cross, this can be taken as an indication that stock prices are likely to be pushed in a downward direction in the near future.

An example chart with the RSI is shown below.

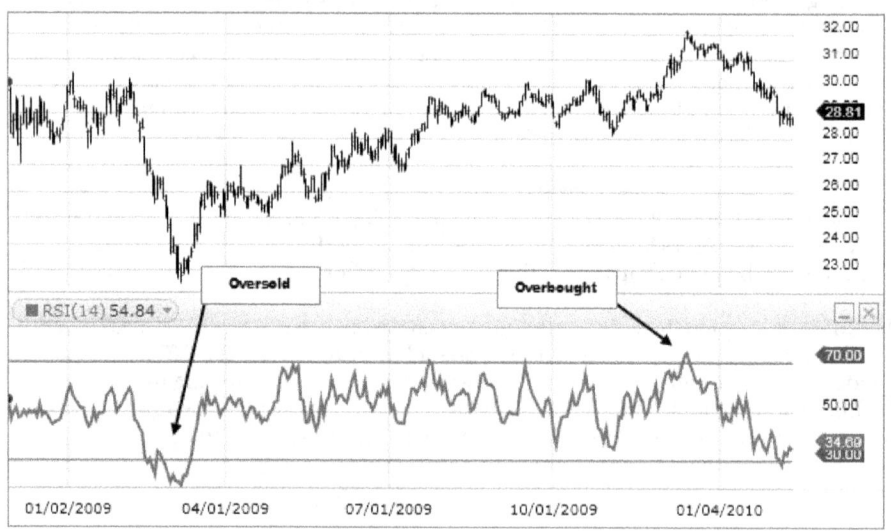

Support and Resistance

The concepts of support and resistance are important for options traders to understand, especially if you are interested in trading iron condors. These concepts are not complicated, so most readers will have no problem grasping them.

In many cases, a stock is not going to be shooting up or crashing to the floor. In fact, over most time periods of the stock market, stocks are going to be bouncing around in the same price range, and possibly gradually increasing or maybe decreasing, but over relatively short time periods staying basically the same. When this happens, we say that the stock is "ranging". The values that the stock prices ranges between are called support and resistance.

Support is the low price level. So, while the stock is ranging, it will dip down to the support price level, but not go below it. After it drops to support it will probably start rising again. You want to look for a price that the stock reaches at least twice over the time frame you are looking at in order to declare that a support price.

Resistance is the upper price level that the stock cannot break above. Again, you want to look for the stock price to move up to the resistance price at least twice, over the time frame. So, while the stock is ranging, it will drop down to support, then bounce around, go up to resistance, then drop back down to support again, and keep repeating this process. Stocks can actually do this for extended time periods. For options traders, when the price drops to resistance, this is a time for those trading call options to enter their positions. Put option traders would sell their positions at this point. When the price goes up to resistance level, then traders investing in call options should sell their positions, while this is a point that you would be looking to enter a position if you were interested in trading put options. The rules are basically pretty simple. We will discuss how support and resistance can be used for iron condors in chapter eight. The chart below shows a stock that enters a ranging period, with support and resistance.

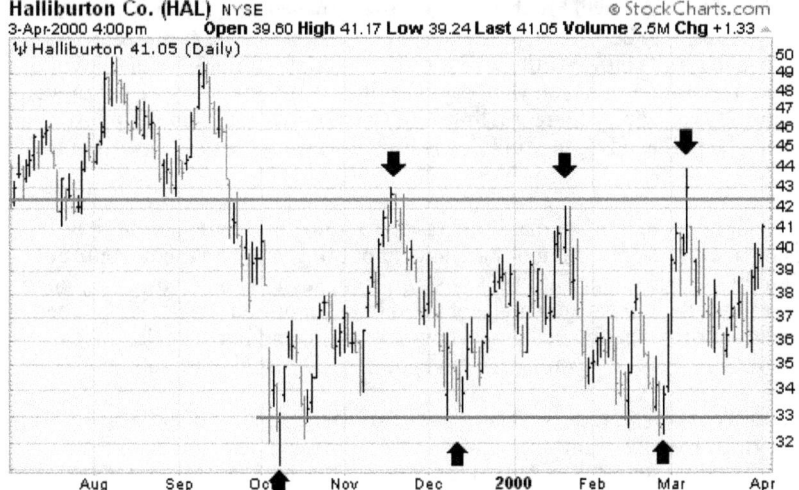

Halliburton Co. (HAL) NYSE   © StockCharts.com
3-Apr-2000 4:00pm   Open 39.60 High 41.17 Low 39.24 Last 41.05 Volume 2.5M Chg +1.33

Breakouts

Breakouts occur when a stock suddenly gains momentum in one direction or the other, and so the price of the stock will break out above resistance or drop below support. In this case, you are likely to be looking at the formation of a new, long-term trend that can help you make profits either with call options or with put options. So, if there is a breakout above resistance, then you want to invest in call options, and ride the upward trend for as long as you can. If there is a breakout to the downside, below support, then you will want to be taking advantage of the ensuing downward trend by investing in put options.

A breakout is not going to happen magically. There is going to be some event that precipitates it. In other words, good or bad news about the company might come out, or there might be a macroeconomic event of some kind, such as an unexpectedly good GDP growth report. So, to take advantage of breakouts, an options trader should be paying close attention to the financial and economic news, and in particular keep an eye on any news about specific companies that you are interested in investing in.

Trendlines

A simple method of analysis that you can use to "trade with the trend", whether it is up or down, is to draw trendlines on your charts. A trendline will help you determine where the stock price is going to end up in the future. Of course, you cannot take this to be an absolute fact, it is only a guide as to what might happen.

To draw a trendline for an upward moving stock price, start at a local low price, and then draw the line upwards, touching the local dips in the curve all the way up. At least 2-3 minima should touch your line. The end of the line (which we are assuming extends past the current price) will give you an estimate of where the price will be at a future date. This image from stockcharts.com illustrates how to draw a trendline.

To draw a trendline for a downward trending price, use the same procedure, but use the local peaks in the price to determine your line.

165

Candlestick Charts

Candlestick charts are another tool that is frequently used by traders, especially day traders and swing traders. They can also be very useful to options traders as well. A candlestick chart breaks up stock data into time frames that you define. This could be five minute intervals, 15 minute intervals, four hour intervals, daily intervals, or many other time frames. A day trader will typically use 5-15 minute interval charts. As an options trader, you might be trading on different time scales, so there isn't a rule that we can use to determine which scale to use. For example, if some news came out about a company, on a single day its stock might be moving strongly in one direction or another, and so you might be using 5-15 minute candlestick charts to track the price movements of the underlying stock. At other times, if you are looking to hold an option over the course of weeks, you might use a daily time frame.

No matter what specific time frame you use, candlestick charts have a common structure. Each time frame is broken down into a "candle" that has a body and two "wicks" or "shadows" sticking out the top and bottom of the body. The color of the body tells you if the price went up or down over the time period of the candle. On most color charts used today, if the price went up, the candle is green. If it went down, it is red. A green candle is called "bullish" and a red candle is called "bearish".

The top of the candle body will represent the closing price for a bullish candle, while the bottom is the opening price. For a bearish candle, these relationships are reversed, and so the top is the opening price, and the bottom is the closing price. The wicks of the candles have the same meaning in both cases. The top wick represents the high price of the trading session, and the bottom wick represents the low price of the trading session.

This is illustrated in the image below.

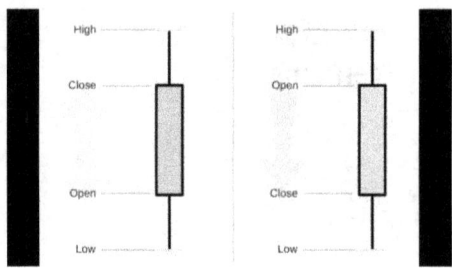

What traders look for are well-known patterns that occur in candlestick charts that indicate trend reversals. For example, if there has been a downward price trend, you are likely to see lots of red (bearish) candlesticks, with prices heading downwards. Then, if you see a large green (bullish) candlestick that completely engulfs the previous bearish candlestick, this is a signal that the price is probably going to reverse.

167

This is illustrated in the image below:

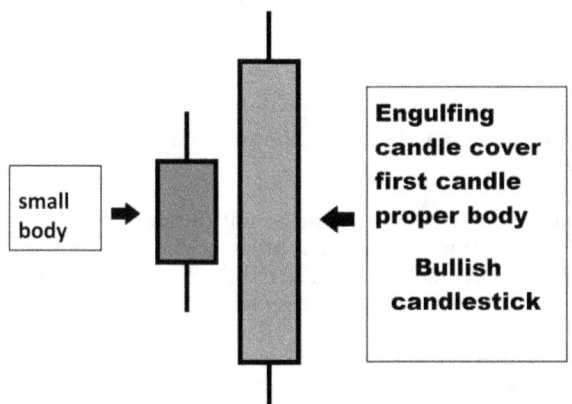

There are a large number of well-known patterns used to study candlestick charts. The topic goes beyond the scope and space in this book, but you can find many online resources and books on stock trading (and videos) that will help you learn to recognize all of the patterns that you need to know in order to utilize candlestick charts in your trading.

The key to using candlestick charts is not to use them in isolation, but to use them together with other tools of technical analysis. For example, I tend to use them with moving averages and the relative strength indicator to make my entry and exit decisions.

Benefits of Technical Analysis
There are many benefits of technical analysis, but the main one I would like to focus on is technical analysis takes emotion out of trading. Of course, this requires a certain level of discipline, but if you use technical analysis to make your decisions rather than just guessing, going on a gut hunch, or trading when you are either panicked or manic, you are more likely to have success in your trades.

Technical analysis has the benefit of providing you with more information, so that you can understand the underlying momentum and therefore make better entry and exit points in your trades as well.

It does have an air about it that is mathematical or scientific, but you shouldn't be put off by that if you are not mathematically inclined. It is not necessary to fully understand the mathematics behind these tools in order to use them, and the rules for using them to make trading decisions are actually fairly easy to learn.

Technical analysis is not something that is going to make you invincible and ensure that every trade is a winner. But something I can tell you is that traders that use technical analysis to one degree or another, on average, tend to do better than traders who don't use it at all.

How deeply you get involved in technical analysis is a matter of personal taste. Does everyone need to use candlestick charts and become familiar with every single candlestick pattern that is supposed to predict a trend reversal? No, they don't. In fact, you are probably better off giving candlestick charts less weight than you give to the moving averages. If there was one tool that I had to recommend for most options traders, it would be using the moving averages to determine your entry and exit points.

Day 6: Let's Trade Options

In this chapter we are going to get into actual options trading. We will look into ways that people select options to trade, and how to look for trades. We will also cover selling options for income. In the next chapter we will cover options strategies used by professional options traders.

Searching for Trades

The first thing to keep in mind about options is that you are going to be looking to trade options on stocks that are going to move in price. While an options trader does not want to be reckless, being excessively conservative is not going to lead to profits either. Remember that a small change in stock price can lead to a large change in the value of an option, putting traders in a position where they can make significant profits. But to get it right, you should be thinking in terms of percentages.

If a stock is trading at $30 a share, a 2% move will mean a $0.60 change in stock price. For the sake of example, let's suppose that we have a strike price of $31 and there are 15 days to expiration, and the implied volatility is 20%. If we buy a call option, the price is $0.15, or $15. If the stock moves 2% that day, then the price of the call option will rise to $32.

Now consider a stock trading at $220 a share. We will consider an option that is out of the money by the same percentage, so we'll choose a strike price of $227. In that case, it would cost us $115 to get a call option. If the stock rose in price by 2%, that means it would rise to $224.40. If that happens, then the call option would rise to $251, so we would have a profit of $136.

Different people are going to have different trading styles, but these examples show that you are going to be in a position to make significant profits going with stocks that have higher share prices. Of course, you could make up for it by buying many options with smaller stock prices, but there are day trading rules that you need to be aware of when taking that approach – and that could cause trouble for your plans (we will discuss this in the next section).

We also have to consider that with a higher priced stock, larger movements in absolute terms are more likely. Remember that a $1 move on the stock might mean a $0.65 move per share for the option or more. This would mean a $65 profit. With a stock with a low share price, such a movement is far less likely. However, you should always check the implied volatility, but once again keeping in mind that less volatility is necessary for high priced stocks to get profits with options.

Another factor to consider is the popularity of a stock. Many stocks that are trading at less than $100 a share are just not that sought out by investors. This will often mean two things. First it might be a lot less likely that they will see the kinds of price movements you need in order to make profits (but that depends), and second it will be harder to get in and out of trades.

The best approach is to go with popular stocks that are $100 or more per share, and that have good values of volatility. Popular index funds are also very good choices.

Keep SPY, DIA, and QQQ in mind to track the S & P 500, Dow Jones Industrial Average, and NASDAQ 100.

We also need to remember that it cuts both ways – you can lose as much money as you can earn. So that means you need to carefully study any stock you are looking to invest in to have a good idea of what direction it's going to move in. If a stock is going to move down, you can always invest in put options. But you need to look at the following factors:

- The volatility of the stock.
- The price of the stock, and the magnitude of 1-2% moves.
- Recent news about the company.
- Current economic conditions.
- Whether there is an upcoming earnings call or product announcement that could cause a large and unpredictable move in the stock price.

Day Trading Rules

Many more conservative readers are going to be tempted to try and earn profits by trading in volume instead of going for a smaller number of options on high priced stocks. If you take this approach, you need to be aware of the day trading rules – and trade options that have different strike prices and expiration dates.

An option on a stock that is the same type, same expiration date, and same strike prices is the same security. That means if you make a large number of trades, it is subject to the day trading rules, and you might not be able to exit your positions at the most prudent time.

The basic day trading rule is that if you buy a stock and sell that same stock before the market closes, that is a day trade. To think in terms of options consider options with the same ticker in the options chain to be a "stock" for the purposes of this rule. It is important to note, because sometimes you have to get out of an option on the same trading day. You might either earn large profits and want to take advantage of it before momentum shifts or you lose value from time decay, or you might need to get out of a losing trade before you get wiped out.

Day trading is strictly regulated by the SEC. You can have 3 day trades in any five day period (five business days, consecutive). Your broker might give you a warning, or at least allow you to track the number of day trades that you have made. You might also get a day trading warning if you attempt to buy a large number of options at once. This is just something to keep in mind, check with your broker for the specific rules for guidance.

A day trader must have a margin account with $25,000 in value (equity + cash). You should also check to see what your brokers rules are in the event that you end up making 4 day trades in a 5-day period.

Selling Call Options

Now we are going to shift gears, and consider selling options for income, rather than buying options hoping to profit by trading. Many traders prefer selling options. Although there are risks, selling options is actually a more reliable approach for

171

earning money than trying to speculate with trading. There is still a level of speculating when you are selling options, but the speculation is one-sided, making it less risky. We will see how this works in a minute.

Covered Call

The simplest way to sell options for income is using covered calls. To sell a covered call, you must own 100 shares of stock for each option that you want to sell. So, if you have been investing in some of your favorite stocks over the years and you have built up some shares, you can start earning money off the shares by selling call options against them.

The strategy involves selling the options with a strike price that is out of the money. If you sell in the money options, while you are going to be able to get a nice payment, your options will be "called away" if they expire in the money, and there is even a risk a buyer might exercise the option before expiration. So, beginning traders are better off selling out of the money options, even though you earn less money.

The money you are paid for selling an option is called the premium. This is analogous to an insurance premium, and many people trading stocks invest in options for the purposes of insurance. This is especially true to get protection against falling stock prices, buying a put option can give you insurance by giving you the out of being able to sell the stock at the strike price of the put in the event that prices drop significantly.

With a covered call, you find the option that you want to sell in the options chain, and then just use the interface of your broker to sell to open the option. You will be credited the amount that the option is trading at the time. If the option expires, and the share price did not put your option in the money, then you will actually be able to take that out as cash.

Breakeven Price

Breakeven price is important to note when selling options. If the share price has not gone above the breakeven price, nobody is going to exercise the option. To take a simple example, if the share price is $100 and it costs $2 to buy the option (per share), then the breakeven price for a call option is $102. So, the stock price has to rise above $102 to make it worth it to a buyer to exercise the option.

For a put option, subtract the price paid for the option to get the breakeven price. For our $100 stock, if a put option costs $2, then the breakeven price is $100- $2 = $98.

Buying an Option Back

One strategy used by traders who sell options, is to reduce the risk of having the option exercised, they will buy the option back before it expires. This will reduce your overall profit, but eliminate the risk that a sudden price movement will put the option in the money (past breakeven) and it will be exercised. Remember that if a call option is exercised, you will be required to sell 100 shares of stock at the strike price. If a put option is exercised, you will be required to buy 100 shares of stock at the strike price. The key to this strategy is time decay. So, if you sell an option for $2 a share or $200, if it is out of the money as it nears expiration it will be worth pennies on the dollar. So, you can buy it back without losing too much income. In the event an option goes in the money and it looks like it is not going to move again in your favor, you can always take a slight loss and buy it back to avoid having to sell the shares.

172

Protected Puts

Another strategy is to sell put options, and if you are only a level 1 or level 2 trader, you can sell a protected put. However, this requires tying up a large amount of capital. To sell a protected put you must have enough money in your account in the form of cash to buy 100 shares of the stock in the event the option is exercised. While this could be a way to earn regular income, it requires a lot of money in proportion to small earnings, and there are better ways to earn money.

Debit Spreads

Now let's consider one of the most popular ways to earn money from selling options, that don't involve having to own the shares of stock or putting up large amounts of cash. This is done using so-called bull and bear spreads, or put and call spreads. We will use the latter terminology.

A spread involves buying and selling two options at the same time. With a credit spread, it is a form of earning income. With a debit spread, you are essentially trading options but reducing the risk. So, let's look at that first.

Consider a call debit spread. With a call debit spread, you will buy an option at a lower strike price, and then sell an option at a higher strike price. The reason that traders do this is that you lower your risk by selling an option at a higher strike price. So, if the lower strike price option expires out of the money and proves to be a losing trade, you still have the premium you received by selling the option with the higher strike price. So, you will lose a lower amount of money than you would have only buying a single call option. This type of trade is entered into simultaneously, that is you buy and sell the 2 call options in a single trade, called a call debit spread. A trader can buy a call option that is in the money, to earn higher profits, and then sell a cheap out of the money call option to mitigate the risk. This strategy is used when you expect the stock price to rise.

You can also invest in a put debit spread. In this case, you buy an in the money put option with a higher strike price, and then mitigate your risk by selling an out of the money put option with a lower strike price. You use this strategy when you expect the stock price to drop.

Note that to trade spreads, you must be a level 3 options trader.

Credit Spreads

Credit spreads are an income generating strategy. The most frequently type of credit spread used is a put credit spread. In this case, you are going to trade 2 out of the money put options at the same time. However, you will sell a put option with a higher strike price, and then buy a put option with a lower strike price.

For a put credit spread to work, all you need is for the stock price to stay above the strike price (less breakeven, technically) of the put option with the higher strike price. What the stock does beyond that is immaterial.

This is a credit, and so your account is credited with premium earned. You will receive a higher payment with the high strike price option than you will have to spend buying the lower strike price option, so this will be a net credit. When the options expire or you close the trade by buying the first option back and selling the option you purchased, you actually have cash in your account. So, this strategy can be used to generate regular income. You can sell credit spreads on a weekly basis, or some traders do it on a monthly or 45 day basis. The longer the time frame, the more premium you can earn. Money is earned from time decay, but even with a week to expiration you can earn significant amounts of money from select stocks. Keep in mind that the longer you stay in a trade, the higher the probability it might go in the money.

Let's consider the case that the stock does go in the money. Suppose that you sell a put option with a strike price of $218 on a stock trading at $220. You would earn a premium of $262, which means that the cost per share is $2.62, and the breakeven price is $218 - $2.62 = $215.38. So, the stock must drop lower than $215.38 before someone will exercise it. However, what would that cost? Suppose the stock drops to $214 a share. Then you would be forced to buy 100 shares at $218 a share. They could then be sold on the open market at $214 a share, so your loss would be $4 a share. But this is mitigated by the $2.62 per share that you got from selling the option, so the total loss is $4 - $2.62 = $1.38 per share, or $138 total.

But this is a spread, so you will have purchased another option as part of the deal. Suppose that for our example, you have purchased a $212 strike price put option. That would have cost you $0.85. When the stock drops to $214, it would actually go up in value to $2.53, even though it is still out of the money. You can sell it to recoup your losses.

Maximum loss for a put credit spread happens when the stock price drops below the strike price of the lower strike price put option, so in this case it would have to drop below $212. The maximum loss is the difference in the strike prices, which for our example would be $218 - $212 = $6 x 100 shares = $600.

Maximum profit is the net credit received. For this example, it would be the $262 received from selling the $218 strike less the $85 received for buying the $212 strike, or $177. If the stock price remains above the higher strike price, you keep the profit.

If stocks or stable or rising, this is a very good strategy for earning income.

The risk of buying and selling stock is not in itself worth worrying about. It all happens automatically. So, if your options go in the money, the broker is going to do the transactions for you. Since the idea here is rising stock prices, some people call this a "bull" credit spread.

If stocks are stable or dropping, you can use the same strategy with call options, using a call credit spread. In that case, you sell a call option with a lower strike price, and buy one with a higher strike price to mitigate your risk. In declining markets or recessions, call credit spreads can be used. Since call credit spreads are used when stock prices are declining, they are called bear credit spreads.

Although you get a credit and you are SELLING a credit spread, you have to cover it with collateral. Your broker will require you to have a certain amount of cash in your account as collateral. The cash will only be used in the case of a loss, it won't be spent otherwise.

Selling Naked Put Options

A simpler trading method is to simply sell one option without buying another one to mitigate risk. Professional traders prefer this method, but you have to open a margin account to do it. This will require a cash deposit of $2,500. You will also have to deposit some collateral cash, and the requirements are higher than what is required for a credit spread. However, it is far less than what is required for a protected put, a small fraction of the money in fact.

Professional traders consider selling naked put options to be a low risk strategy. Financial advisors are going to tell you differently but the reality is they don't know what they are talking about. If you sell out of the money put options – while carefully studying the stocks and macroeconomic situation – it is actually a simple matter to earn profits most of the time. Remember that financial advisors are motivated to get you to invest in mutual funds and other products, so they don't like the competition. Second, the buyback strategy is used by professional options traders when selling naked put options. That means you have to be paying close attention to your trades, and then be ready to buy back any options that go in the money. When you buy back an option that you have sold, your obligations are removed.

Each broker will have a formula that determines the amount of cash you must put up as collateral. Check with your specific broker to learn the details. So, the process of selling naked put options involves depositing enough cash to cover the collateral requirements, then finding the option with the strike price that you want to sell. Brokers will tell you the probability of profit for each strike price. Professional options traders recommend selling put options with a probability of profit of 70% or higher. So, think about the number – over the course of two years if you sell 100 put options, that means 70 of them will earn profits, and 30 of them would not. That doesn't necessarily mean you would lose money, if you are on top of things you would be buying back the 30 options that were losing trades, not waiting to the last minute.

To sell naked options, you must be a level 4 trader.

You can also sell naked call options. The principles are the same, but when you sell naked put options, you are going to be doing so expecting the stock price to stay above the strike price of your option. So, you are going to sell naked put options when you are neutral or bullish on the stock. For naked call options, you will sell a naked call option when you expect the stock price to be neutral or drop, so it will remain below the strike price. So, you sell naked call options when you are bearish.

It is possible to make a high income, on the order of $500,000 to $1 million or more a year, selling naked options. But it is not without risk, so be sure to get some trading experience and do a lot of study before you embark on a career selling options. But again, remember that most professional traders sell either naked put options or iron condors (to be covered in the next chapter).

Day 7: Options Strategies

In this chapter we are going to review the most popular options strategies that allow you to earn money in unusual situations. These include strangles, straddles, and the iron butterfly among others. You must be a level 3 options trader to use these strategies.

Strangles and Straddles

This type of strategy is used when the stock is expected to make a large pricing move, but you don't know the direction that the stock will move. It involves buying a call and put option together in a single trade. A strangle involves setting a bounding range for the expected stock movement, using different strike prices for the put and call option. A lower strike price is used for the put option, while a higher strike price is used for the call option. Breakeven price is the breakeven price for the call option if the stock rises, or the breakeven price for the put option if the stock drops.

As an example, if the share price of a stock was $100 but it was expected to make a big move, you could set up a strangle with a $105 call option and a $95 put option. If the stock prices fails to move either above the call option strike price or below the put option strike price, you will lose money on the trade. The maximum possible loss is the cost of buying the options.

The strategy is considered neutral because it will make profits if the stock moves up (strongly) or down (strongly). You will invest in this type of strategy when you expect a large move in the stock, so for example many traders buy strangles prior to an earnings call. Most earnings calls result in big price movements of the stock, but prior to the call you aren't sure which direction it will actually move.

The strike prices selected for the call and put option will be out of the money. Both options will have the same expiration date.

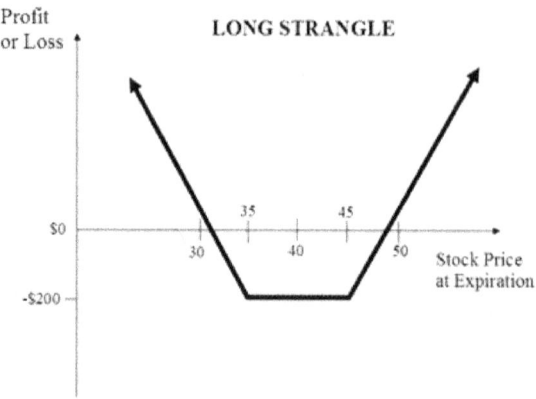

Maximum profit on the upside is theoretically unlimited, but it will depend how far the stock price moves above the strike of the call option. If that happens, the put option expires worthless, and your profit selling the call option less the cost of buying the put option is your net profit. If the stock price drops, maximum profit would occur in the extremely unlikely case that it dropped to zero, less the cost of the call option. If the stock price moves to any level below the breakeven price of the put option, you can earn a profit.

A straddle is used for the same purpose, but in this case we set the strike prices of the call and put option to the same value, and both options will have the same expiration date. With a straddle you want the stock price to move off the strike price used in either direction.

Iron Condor

An iron condor is one of the most popular options strategies. This is an income producing strategy, and an iron condor is sold for a net credit (keep this is mind, there is a lot of misinformation about iron condors). An iron condor is sold using a call credit spread, and a put credit spread, all in the same trade. The two options with inner strike prices will be sold. So, for example, suppose that a stock is trading at $200 a share. You could sell a call option with a strike price of $205, and buy a call option with a strike price of $210. Simultaneously, you would sell a put option with a $195 strike price, and buy a put option with a $190 strike price.

As long as the stock price stays in between the inner strike prices – ranging between $195 and $205 in our example – you will make a profit. So, an iron condor is used when you expect the stock price is not going to change very much over the lifetime of the options. All options used in an iron condor have the same expiration date.

To pick your strike prices, determine where support and resistance are. You want to set the strike price of the put option you sell a little bit above the support price, and set the strike price of the call option you sell a little bit below the resistance price. Then set the outer strike prices slightly above the resistance price level for the purchased call option and below the support price level for the purchased put option.

Many traders make a full-time living strictly selling iron condors. The chart has the following form.

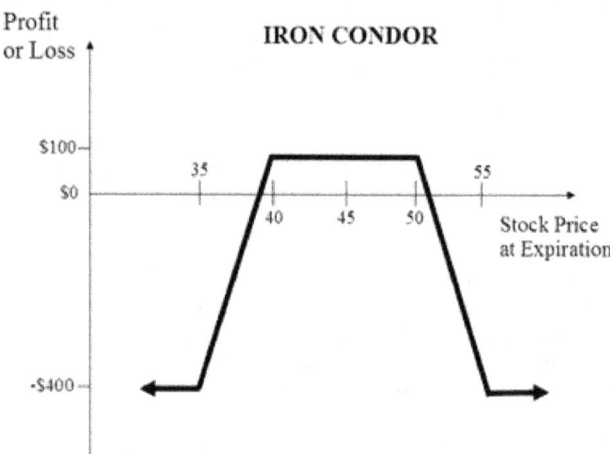

Profit or Loss

IRON CONDOR

$100—
$0

35
40   45   50
55

Stock Price
at Expiration

-$400—

You will receive a net credit for the call credit spread, and a net credit for the put credit spread. The total credit received is your maximum profit. If the stock remains in between the inner strike prices, this is when you will earn profits.

One advantage of the iron condor is that losses are also capped. The maximum loss, should the stock move to the upside, is the difference in strike prices of the two call options. Should the stock move downward, the maximum loss is the difference between the strike prices of the put options. Using our example, here would be a $5 loss (per share – total $500) if the stock moved below $190, or above $210.

Iron Butterfly

An iron butterfly is a less popular way to set this up, since it creates a narrow range for the stock. In the case of an iron butterfly, you set your inner strike prices the same. So, for example, using a stock trading at $200, we could sell a call option and a put option with a $200 strike price, and then buy a call option with a $205 strike price, and buy a put option with a $195 strike price. Losses will be incurred if the stock price goes above the $205 strike of the upper call or below the $195 strike of the put.

Equity Collar

This is a strategy used to hedge risk. It is used on a long stock position that you have, and this is used by large traders. So, to use this strategy you would have a large number of shares of some stock. If you are uncertain about the direction of the stock that you own, you could setup an equity collar to hedge your risk with put and call options. You set it up by buying an equal number of put and call options with strike prices above the share price for the call options and strike prices below the share price for put options. The options will all have the same expiration date. If the share price moves above the call strike price, you will earn profits on the call options and the put options will expire worthless. If the stock price moves below the put options, the call options will expire worthless. You can exercise the put options and sell your stock at a price that is higher than the market price, or sell the put options for a profit and keep your stock.

Short Gut

A short gut is a less popular options strategy that involves selling a call and a put option simultaneously. You sell the two options with the same expiration month, but not necessarily the same expiration date. First you sell a call option at a certain strike price, and then you sell a put option with a higher strike price. Maximum losses are uncapped if the stock price moves in either direction, so you are hoping the stock price will stay the same. Maximum profit is equal to the premiums received from selling the options. This is a little used strategy and you must be a level 4 options trader to use it, and you must have enough cash in your account to cover selling the two options (cash as collateral).

Long Gut
A long gut involves buying a call option and buying a put option with a higher strike price. In this case, you are hoping to make profit from the stock moving in either direction, so it is someone analogous to a strangle, but you are doing it with the strike prices of the call and put reversed. If the stock price moves up, you will make money from the call but lose money on the put, if the strike price moves down, you will make money on the put and lose on the call.

Synthetic Strategies
Synthetic strategies are obscure and rarely used by small traders. To make a synthetic put, you must have a large margin account. To set it up you will short the stock, so you will borrow shares of stock from the broker and sell them on the market, hoping to buy them back at a lower price. Then you will buy a call option on the same stock. If the stock price rises, you will make a profit on the call option to help offset the loss of having to buy the shares back at a higher price (if you borrow shares from the broker, you have to buy them back and return them to the broker at some point). If the stock price drops as expected, you will lose money on the call option which will expire worthless, but you will make the expected profit from shorting the stock, and you can buy it back at the lower share price, return the shares to the broker, and then the profit from doing that less the cost of the call option is your net profit. So, this involves shorting stock using a call option as insurance.

Conclusion

Thank you for making it through to the end of *Options Trading Crash Course*, let's hope it was informative and able to provide you with all of the tools you need to achieve your goals whatever they may be.

Now that you are familiar with all the different types of options and trading strategies, it is time to get started. Work out your plan for the first three months of options trading and open a brokerage account to get started with your trading.

Remember to always keep up with your education. By adopting an approach of continuing education with options trading you can ensure that you are able to build a winning trading strategy!

Finally, if you found this book useful in any way, a review on Amazon is always appreciated!

CPSIA information can be obtained
at www.ICGtesting.com
Printed in the USA
LVHW020545301120
672994LV00012B/295

9 781914 176296